About Island Press

Since 1984, the nonprofit organization Island Press has been stimulating, shaping, and communicating ideas that are essential for solving environmental problems worldwide. With more than 1,000 titles in print and some 30 new releases each year, we are the nation's leading publisher on environmental issues. We identify innovative thinkers and emerging trends in the environmental field. We work with world-renowned experts and authors to develop cross-disciplinary solutions to environmental challenges.

Island Press designs and executes educational campaigns, in conjunction with our authors, to communicate their critical messages in print, in person, and online using the latest technologies, innovative programs, and the media. Our goal is to reach targeted audiences—scientists, policy makers, environmental advocates, urban planners, the media, and concerned citizens—with information that can be used to create the framework for long-term ecological health and human well-being.

Island Press gratefully acknowledges major support from The Bobolink Foundation, Caldera Foundation, The Curtis and Edith Munson Foundation, The Forrest C. and Frances H. Lattner Foundation, The JPB Foundation, The Kresge Foundation, The Summit Charitable Foundation, Inc., and many other generous organizations and individuals.

The opinions expressed in this book are those of the author(s) and do not necessarily reflect the views of our supporters.

BICYCLE
CITY

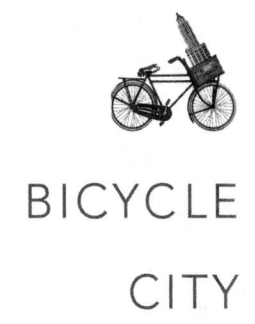

BICYCLE CITY

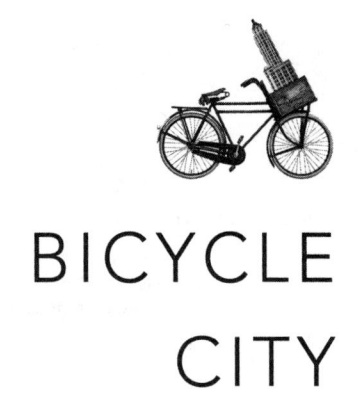

Riding the Bike Boom to a Brighter Future

Dan Piatkowski

ISLANDPRESS | Washington | Covelo

© 2024 Daniel Piatkowski

All rights reserved under International and Pan-American Copyright Conventions. No part of this book may be reproduced in any form or by any means without permission in writing from the publisher: Island Press, 2000 M Street, NW, Suite 480-B, Washington, DC 20036-3319.

Library of Congress Control Number: 2023950594

All Island Press books are printed on environmentally responsible materials.

Manufactured in the United States of America
10 9 8 7 6 5 4 3 2 1

Keywords: bike infrastructure; bikeshare; bike tourism; biking; cargo bike; car-lite city; COVID-19; cycling; e-bike; electrification; e-scooter; gravel riding; inclusive transportation; Lincoln, Nebraska; micromobility; mobility; open street; Oslo, Norway; pandemic bike boom; shared mobility; sustainable transportation; tactical urbanism; transit; transportation; Vision Zero

*For Melissa, Petra, and Phoebe.
And Dale and Zombie.*

Two wheels in motion,
Weave through mechanical beasts,
The city sings out.

—Eric North

CONTENTS

Preface xiii

Acknowledgments xxiii

Introduction The Bicycle City 1

Chapter 1 The Pandemic and the Bicycle Boom 21

Chapter 2 E-Bikes: Changing the Game 39

Chapter 3 Cargo Bikes: Big, Slow, and Revolutionary 51

Chapter 4 Micromobility: Smaller, Cheaper, and More Fun than Cars 71

Chapter 5 The Urban Bias in Bicycling 87

Conclusion The Path to the Bicycle City 103

Epilogue 123

Notes 127

About the Author 161

PREFACE

> "I wouldn't live there if you paid me to."
> —Talking Heads, "The Big Country"

I HAD ALWAYS THOUGHT THAT WE, AS A SOCIETY, could do what it takes to improve our cities. But I was gradually giving up on the idea that we could do so in time to preserve a livable climate. I was falling into the trap of utopia as a naïve fantasy rather than a uniting trajectory. It took a dramatic and life-changing move, to a new country, a new lifestyle, and a new job, to change my mind.

I research and teach urban planning, and after a decade of doing so at universities in the United States, I was looking for a change. Then, in the winter of 2022, I was offered a job at a university in Oslo, Norway. My family and I decided to go for it: to move from Lincoln, Nebraska, to Oslo. My wife and I were excited about the prospect of a new adventure for us and our daughters: the chance to experience a new way of life, a new culture, another language. When most people think of Norway, they probably think of fjords and Vikings, possibly the Winter Olympics, or maybe even Norway's outsize impact on heavy metal music.[1]

Beyond the stereotypes, Norway is gaining attention for its capital city's increases in traffic safety, reductions in greenhouse gas emissions, and overall livability. Over the past ten years, Oslo has become one of a handful of cities leading the world in urban sustainability. In my new job there, I would be teaching and researching how transportation plays a role in Oslo's sustainability goals.

So many European cities, but especially those in northern Europe and Scandinavia, feel like alternative realities for what American cities could be. As an American urban planner, and a cyclist, I spent a lot of time looking across the Atlantic. It can be really hard to keep from feeling disillusioned and hopeless about Americans' inability to quit cars. In my research, I study how to make bicycling a viable mode of transportation for more people, but you don't need to be an expert to understand why so few people ride bikes in the United States. Moving to Oslo felt like a chance to flip the problem on its head; I could learn firsthand why so many people ride bikes in cities in other countries.

I've always loved cities. Before I ever thought about bicycles, I thought about cities. They were the backdrop to, and sometimes the subject of, my favorite books, movies, and music. But the cities I was fascinated by were not like where I lived. I grew up in the suburbs of Phoenix, Arizona, during the 1980s and 1990s. In 1980, the population of the Phoenix metropolitan area was about 1.4 million people. Today, Phoenix has nearly quadrupled in population and is home to about 4.7 million people living predominantly in single-family-home suburbs spread out over more than five hundred square miles of desert. I can look back and point out the myriad problems with suburban sprawl, but at the time I never thought about it.

I thought of New York as the pinnacle of American urbanism, and I wanted to experience it, so I moved there in 2001. Not surprisingly, it was an expensive and difficult place to live. When I wasn't working, I borrowed my roommate's 1970s road bike, a hand-me-down from his father. It was surreal to experience the city from a new perspective, being part of the flow of traffic but also separate from it. (At the time, New York City had very little bicycle infrastructure, so cyclists were left to make their own rules.) I spent more and more of my free time on that bike. It made sense. I didn't have much money, and going for a bike ride was free.

After months of no success in finding a decent job, I decided to become a bike messenger. Messengers got to be outside and ride all day, and they seemed so cool. My only prior experience as a cyclist, however, was riding to my suburban elementary school. I learned quickly what should have been obvious: being a bike messenger is a really hard job. It requires a combination of skill, talent, and physical ability, none of which I had. The job was too hard for me. I felt like a tourist in the gritty world of urban cycling.

But it did give me a new perspective on bikes. I had never necessarily thought of bikes as just toys; in fact, I had never really thought about bikes at all before trying to be a bike messenger. I discovered they were a cheap and flexible connector between the most vibrant and exciting places in New York City. By extension, I started to think about the potential for bicycles in less dense places, like the suburbs I grew up in. From there, it was a relatively direct path to becoming an urban planner.

I spent a little more time in New York City after my failed attempt at riding a bike for a living. I got a job at a bike shop and learned a lot about the bike industry, selling bikes, and fixing bikes. Eventually, I made a career combining my love of cities with my love of bikes. I moved back to Arizona and went to graduate school for urban planning. I then worked as a planner in New Mexico and Colorado before earning a PhD in design and planning and going into academia. My first faculty job was at Savannah State University in Savannah, Georgia—the oldest planned city in the United States. The Oglethorpe Plan, from 1733, dictated the gridded pattern of the historic downtown, with homes and businesses built around public squares.

Every weekend, I saw Savannah's downtown overrun by tourists flocking to good urbanism (and the city's lax drinking laws). Millions of people visit Savannah every year to experience one of the best examples of human-centered city design in the United States. But Savannah's downtown is an island of urbanism in a sea of automobile dependence.

After a few years, I moved from Savannah to a faculty position at the University of Nebraska–Lincoln and saw a different facet of American urbanism. Lincoln is indicative of a newer and more widespread American urbanism. The city was built primarily in the nineteenth and twentieth centuries, straddling the pre- and post-automobile eras. This is a history shared with dozens of cities and towns across the United States. Therefore, solutions to auto dependence in places like Lincoln are generalizable to millions of Americans. Lincoln had challenges similar to Savannah's in terms of auto dependence, but it also has an impressive network of bike paths connecting cyclists to the gravel riding that is now synonymous with cycling in the Midwest.

Everywhere I have lived, I have thought about the potential for improvement—the potential for changing the trajectory away from cars and toward people. I have studied the type of infrastructure and policies necessary to get people out of their cars. I have studied what needs to happen to make vibrant places, built on a backbone of great public transit, where people can go about their lives without needing to drive. I always assumed that I needed to be more patient. After all, cities are dynamic places, and that dynamism is typically measured in decades.

But Oslo is unique in that it is relatively new to the "bicycle city" game, and it has made me rethink my assumptions. First, becoming a bicycle city is not the number one priority for Oslo. Oslo initiated a plan focused on "car-free livability" in order to become more "people centric."[2] While not the priority, bicycling had—and continues to have—a significant role in realizing that goal. Prior to coming to Oslo, I had thought very little about bicycles as an intermediary between where we are (i.e., auto dependent) and where we want to be (i.e., people centric). Understanding that was foundational to this book.

Second, Oslo has changed how I think about the time it takes for cities to change. I assumed that in the absence of catastrophic events like wars or natural disasters, change is slow. Oslo has historically been relatively auto dependent (compared with European cities), but everything changed in the past decade. From 2014 to 2020, there was an almost 80 percent increase in bicycling in Oslo.[3] This is what inspired me to move halfway around the world and reboot my career in a new country. This is what inspired me to write a book about how US cities can do the same.

I have no plans to leave Norway, but I have also not left the United States behind. Throughout the ups and downs of daily life in a new and foreign place, I inevitably make comparisons with home, both good and bad. As a foreigner in Norway, I am also partially defined by my nationality. As a result, I think a lot about being American. In some ways, moving abroad has made me feel even more American. Today, I feel as if I have a foot in each place. Despite my change of address, I care deeply about my home country and the trajectory of American cities.

Utopia Is a Myth

I have thought a lot about the concept of utopia as I've worked on this book. It's a concept that is hard to avoid when thinking about cities. I study cities professionally, with the explicit goal of determining how our cities can improve our lives and the planet. I came by this profession from a childhood spent in urban spaces that did the opposite. Like millions of Americans, I grew up in suburbia—itself the flawed manifestation of utopianism. It is clear today that our cities are in desperate need of help. For me, that sense of desperation easily morphs into utopian dreams of more perfect places.

Utopia is hard to pin down. As I try to think through exactly what my near-utopian vision of a better city is, I struggle to bring it into focus. It is easier to focus first on broad strokes. It means places that are holistically better, that allow all of us to live more complete and full lives. There are basic requirements for functional places. The places we live should be safe and welcoming to all. The places we live must also be healthy and sustainable and increasingly resilient against the growing uncertainties of the future, both human and environmental.

Achieving this baseline for places, let alone reaching some utopian peak, can feel impossible. This is usually where the dreaming ends. This is when the adults in the room remind us that the world doesn't work that way and anyone who thinks otherwise is, at best, hopelessly naïve. But that is a recipe for preserving the status quo. The difference between possible and impossible is just what we expect versus what is unexpected. During the past few years, all of us have had our expectations shattered, our habits upended.

Despite all of the tragedy and turmoil the COVID-19 pandemic has brought, it has also shattered our understanding of what is possible and what is impossible. The initial prognosis was bleak for cities, but as they recover, cities are trying to redefine how they function and who they serve. There is a path forward for making the places we live work for everyone and for the planet. I have been called naïve more than once. It's an insult usually followed by a list of reasons why the real world is different and we don't live in some perfect utopia where anything is possible and everything works out fine.

But I am not the first person, and certainly not the first student of good urbanism, to be called naïve. The study of cities by architects, planners, designers, engineers, and politicians is founded on the idea that we can improve our lives by improving the cities we live in. It may be naïve and utopian, but it is not new. The study of cities is founded on this utopian idea, if for no other reason than that the opposite—to study cities for the purpose of making our lives worse—would be insane. The foundational ideas about urban form and function are rooted in betterment.

Ebenezer Howard, founder of the Garden Cities movement in the late nineteenth century, wrote the book *Garden Cities of To-Morrow: A Peaceful Path to Real Reform*,[4] detailing his vision. He imagined a near-perfect town: self-sustaining communities that balanced town living with country amenities in orderly and connected nodes surrounding a central (larger) city. The goal was to determine "how to make our Garden City experiment the stepping-stone to a higher and better form of industrial life generally throughout the country."[5] Those following Howard's utopian dream made many missteps. In the twentieth century, inspired by the potential for the automobile to reshape cities, people such as the Swiss-born French architect Le Corbusier drafted detailed designs for radiant, orderly cities—cities perfectly tailored to the needs of cars, at the expense of residents.

Cities are aspirational places, and the origins of utopia as an idea are tied to this notion. Utopia is an old idea. Almost five hundred years ago, Thomas More coined the term in his book *Utopia*,[6] describing a fictional perfect island-state. The book goes into detail describing this society, functioning perpetually in its flawless state. It lays the groundwork for the idea that a utopia is a real possibility—an end goal for civilization in form and function. In More's utopia, there is no private property, and the possession of money, gems, and precious metals is frowned upon. Gold, for example, is so loathed as a symbol of excess that is used only for chamber pots or to shackle slaves.

Yet More's utopia is far from perfect; the most glaring example of this is the presence of slavery on the island. More was the originator of an idea that we cannot seem to give up. Utopia is an alluring concept, but that is probably because it is a fantasy that we humans have never been able to realize.

Imagining a perfect society in its end state is a theoretical exercise. In the real world, societies don't magically appear, cast in amber and self-sustaining in a static state in perpetuity. Places, people, and systems change and evolve.

Technologies are introduced, environments change, demographics change, and political dynamics shift. The concept of utopia still applies when talking about improving the places we live and the systems that maintain them, just not as an end-state, static utopia. For the purposes of this book, I am inspired by a more modern take on utopia: utopia as a method, a process that is aspirational but also grounded in reality.[7]

Science fiction excels at offering glimpses into alternative futures, launching us from reality into the unknown. While dystopian science fiction, from zombie apocalypses to alien invasions, tends to get most of the attention, there is more to the genre. There is an entire subgenre of science fiction, critical utopias, that grapple with the concept, and the realities, of utopia.

In 1974, Ursula K. Le Guin published *The Dispossessed*. The first edition included the subtitle *The Magnificent New Epic of an Ambiguous Utopia*.[8] Le Guin was inspired by anarchist thinkers and utopian ideas. The subtitle of the book references the departure from utopia as Thomas More's fictional island and into a reality in which people live in a system that is working at becoming increasingly utopian.[9] The book is about two cultures on two planets, one an anarchist utopia, the other a capitalist system. Everyone works for the common good in the anarchist utopian society, eschewing private property.

The main character in Le Guin's novel, a man named Shevek, is a brilliant scientist who finds that, for a variety of reasons, his utopian home is not perfect. For example, Shevek is frustrated that in service to his community, he needs to put his research aside to work for the common good doing manual labor. Eventually, he journeys to the capitalist planet to continue his research. In the capitalist world, Shevek is disgusted by the materialism and exploitation inherent in the society. He eventually returns to his home, secure in the realization that it is not perfect, but it is revolutionary in its utopian goal. As Le Guin wrote, the utopian society was "conceived as a permanent revolution, and revolution begins in the thinking mind."[10] It is a fantastic book that I think about frequently. The most interesting thing about the book, to me, is that it puts the reader into a functioning utopia. Doing so demystifies utopia and makes it real.

We all put our pants on one leg at a time, and Le Guin imagines that it is no different in utopia. The minutiae of daily life, the conflicts, struggles, and tensions, exist anywhere. We can never escape the more self-sabotaging aspects of human nature, but we can place them within a more equitable and just society, in a place that functions in greater harmony with its surroundings.[11]

The *Star Trek* series is based on a similar idea. Underneath the corny dialogue and cheesy makeup, the show is built on critical utopianism. *Star Trek*, including all the various movies and television shows, is based in a fictional world in which there was some kind of terrible war, famine, and environmental destruction on Earth, but in the end humanity survived. In so doing, humanity moved to a post-scarcity future where no one goes without food and a more perfect social and political system recognizes everyone.[12] But the world of *Star Trek* is not perfect. The entire franchise is built on the struggles, wars, and turmoil in the universe, despite everything the characters have going for them. Despite transporters and warp drives, everyone still puts their pants on one leg at a time.

This is the part of utopia, as a concept, that I am interested in: the ambition to improve the places we live in ways that meaningfully advance shared goals like sustainability and equity. I've changed my own definition of utopia from a perfect end state to a process of betterment.

It is much more revolutionary to question the process behind a system than to simply espouse a perfect future, born fully formed. It explains why so much critical utopian literature came out of the social movements of the 1960s and 1970s and focused on dismantling prevailing hierarchies and gender norms.[13]

Science fiction has a way of making a proposition and digging into it, exposing where it leads. Dystopian science fiction tends to get most of the attention in popular culture. But stories about evading zombies or fighting aliens don't offer much insight into pathways to brighter futures. There is a Wikipedia page dedicated to existing technologies predicted by science fiction. It is a fun list, but it reduces the genre to novelty. William Gibson, the celebrated Canadian-American science fiction writer who coined the term "cyberspace" and helped establish the dystopian cyberpunk subgenre of science fiction in the 1980s, is credited multiple times on that list, most notably for predicting the internet and virtual reality. To quote Gibson, "I think the least important thing about science fiction for me is its predictive capacity."[14]

The tradition of critical utopian literature is a tradition of deconstructing the idea of utopia and reframing it as a living thing: a process rather than an end point. The goal for Le Guin, and authors like her, is to question what utopia is and what it would be like to live there—and, in so doing, to inspire people to think beyond the status quo. They have inspired my way of thinking about the bicycle and the process of creating our future cities.[15] The answer is always a messy path, never offering a fully formed or perfect end point.

ACKNOWLEDGMENTS

IT IS HARD TO KNOW WHERE TO START when I think of all the people I would like to thank for helping make this book a reality. For that, I am profoundly grateful. The list needs to start with Heather Boyer at Island Press. In the most real of ways, this book would not have happened without her. She shepherded the book from initial concept to final product. I am perpetually thankful for her insights, perspective, and hard work.

Next, I want to thank Josh Bernstein. Josh has been a writer for as long as I've known him and was the first person I spoke to about the possibility of writing this book. In addition to his advice on the book, I owe it to Josh for inadvertently setting me on the career path that led to this point. Twenty years ago, we were roommates in Brooklyn. I was new to the city, and Josh suggested I borrow his bike to explore it. The bike was his dad's old ten-speed from the 1970s, and I can still remember what it felt like riding through Prospect Park. I can trace a direct line from taking that first ride in Brooklyn in 2001 to sitting in my office in Oslo in 2023. It is fitting that when I first considered writing this book, my first call was to Josh.

I would also like to thank all of the experts, advocates, professionals, and friends whose ideas helped to shape this book. I could not have written this book without a long list of incredible people who were happy to talk with me and were so generous with their time—and everyone who I was never able to connect with, due to crazy schedules and time zone differences, but who nonetheless actively inspired and shaped key facets of the book. In no particular order, that list includes Annie Folck, Cameron Bennett, Jill Warren, Norman Garrick, Jesse Poore, Jim Malmgren, Jos Sluijsmans, Meredith

Glaser, Kevin Klinkenberg, Bill Nesper, Claudia Folska, Jocelyn Vande Velde, Corey Godfrey, Erik Eagleman, Noa Banayan, Chris Nolte, Sam Starr, Torrance Strong, Kari Anne Solfjeld Eid, Anine Hartmann, Terje Elvsaas, Peter Koonce, Justin Bristol, tamika l. butler, Ben Quinn, Calvin Thigpen, and Lelac Almagor.

A special note of gratitude to John Simmerman. He is a tireless advocate whose work with the *Active Towns* podcast was an inspiration for this book. John was also kind enough to connect me with so many of the fascinating people I had the opportunity to speak with for the book.

Moving to Norway was the catalyst for this book in many ways. Upon arriving I was, and I continue to be, inspired by Oslo, the city and the people who call it home. There's an unfortunate stereotype that Norwegians can seem cold or unfriendly, but in my experience it is entirely untrue. The ideas in this book are a direct result of so many insightful conversations with so many people at places such as Whee!, Asplan Viak, Rambøll, Norconsult, the Norwegian Institute of Transport Economics (TØI), Statens Vegvesen, Ruter, Beta Mobility, Syklistenes Landsforening, Oslo Metropolitan University (OsloMet), and the City of Oslo. Specifically (and in addition to being interviewed for this book), I would like to thank Terje Elvsaas, Kari Anne Solfjeld Eid, and Anine Hartmann for their feedback on chapter drafts and for sharing images for the book. I would also like to thank Sondre Bjørgum for the many impromptu motivational conversations that kept me writing.

This work also would not have been possible without the support of my colleagues John Östh, Claudia van der Laag, Chaoru Lu, Marit Sandvik, and many, many others. We all began working together remotely and across continents as I waited for borders to open and visas to be approved so my family and I could finally get to Oslo. Every day on my walk or ride to work, I think about how lucky I am for having the opportunity to work with so many talented people and to count them as friends. I would also like to acknowledge Hallgrim Hjelmbrekke, one of the best bosses I ever had and whose enthusiasm for Norway is infectious, and of course Zacharias Andreadakis, who has helped me so much in navigating the confusion of moving to a new country and getting settled.

Advocacy work is hard work. Effective advocacy means rolling with the punches and keeping your eyes on the prize, no matter how far off in the distance it might be. In addition to being difficult, advocacy work is often thankless. I learned early in my career that successful compromise means no one is happy. Additionally, the vast majority of advocates work for what they love in their spare time for no money. Despite the challenges, advocates stick with it, and their work is instrumental in making lasting and meaningful change in our communities. I have learned from and been inspired by the work of countless advocates for walking, cycling, and active living. In Georgia, that list includes Bike Walk Savannah, Healthy Savannah, and Georgia Bikes. In Nebraska, the list includes Bike Walk Nebraska, BicycLincoln, Trails Have Our Respect (THOR), the Pirate Cycling League, and the Goldenrod Pastries team. In Arizona, it includes the Tempe Bicycle Action Group. In Colorado, it includes Bicycle Colorado and Colorado Bike Law. And nationally, it includes PeopleForBikes and the League of American Bicyclists. In Norway, that list includes Syklistenes Landsforening; and in Europe, the International Cargo Bike Festival and the European Cyclists' Federation.

The way that I think about cities, transport, and cycling has been influenced by a long list of scholars. Throughout my career, some of them have been mentors to me. I would first like to thank Wes Marshall for his mentorship and friendship, without which I would not be doing this work today. I would also like to thank Zhenghong Tang, Deden Rukmana, Kevin Krizek, Susan Handy, Melissa Bopp, Itzhak Benenson, Norman Garrick, Reid Ewing, Ralph Buehler, and Jeremy Németh for their frequent mentorship, for their brilliant scholarship, and for continuing to respond to my calls and emails. I owe this fantastic and strange career to all of you.

For always being unironically awesome people, I would like to thank my friends, in particular, Brian Stolfa, Brian Ellis, Dan Roche, Dan McClary, Eric North, Jim Malmgren, Cameron Gridley, Karl Smith, and Illya Riske.

Finally, I owe my deepest gratitude to my family: to my parents and grandparents for showing me from a young age that the world is big and full of wonder; to my mom and dad for teaching me to seize the day; to my brother for being my oldest friend; and to my wife and children, whose love and support are the foundation for everything I am.

My children inspire me to work toward a better future. One of my greatest joys in life is learning about the world from them. I apply their perspectives and lessons daily to my work, and they have shaped this book. Specifically, I would like to thank Petra for reminding me to keep asking questions and never to settle for incomplete answers. And I would like to thank Phoebe for showing me that curiosity is a physical act, requiring both strength and force of will. Most important, thank you to Melissa: our life together has been more adventurous than either one of us ever imagined. None of it would have been possible without your partnership, patience, and love.

Introduction

The Bicycle City

> "Every time I see an adult on a bicycle,
> I no longer despair for the future of the human race."
> —H. G. Wells

IN HIS 1896 BOOK *The Wheels of Chance: A Bicycling Idyll*, H. G. Wells told the story of a young man learning to ride a bicycle, which was a new invention at the time. After he had spent a day successfully learning to ride, "a new delight was in his eyes, quite over and above the pleasure of rushing through the keen, sweet, morning air. He reached out his thumb and twanged his bell out of sheer happiness."

Freedom, joy, exhilaration, even transcendence. This is the aspirational language of bicycles. Bikes are not just for getting around or for getting exercise; they mediate our experience of places. A bicycle changes how we experience our cities, and in so doing it can help us to unlock the possibilities inherent in the places we live.

The places we live desperately need our help. From small towns to major metropolitan areas, our cities are struggling under the weight of decades of automobile-centric development. We are left with homogeneous and redundant collections of strip malls and parking lots. These places are inequitable, bad for the planet, and bad for our physical and mental health. The places we live can better suit our needs as humans, but we need to free ourselves from the car. This does not necessarily require banishing cars from cities, but it does mean no longer relying on them. We need to create a *car-lite* urban future, and bicycles can help us get there. This is more than just a narrative—the facts support it. Tracing the Dutch or the Danish approach to bicycle urbanism demonstrates the power of bicycles as change agents.

The conventional wisdom is that change takes time, but time is no longer on our side. If we are to address the climate crisis to preserve a livable planet for today, as well as for future generations, our cities need to change quickly. I wrote this book because I believe that it is possible to transform our cities to meet our needs and those of the planet. We can do it in time to avert the worst effects of global warming. And we can do it with the bicycle.

We are at a unique moment in the history of cities, an inflection point that can determine the fate of the planet, whether through concerted action or continued inaction. In this book, I have tried to capture the moment, the knowledge, the lived experience, and the lessons of right now to chart a path to a brighter future.

Three recent developments demonstrate that today is different and the bicycle is different: (1) the advent of e-bike technology and the ubiquity of shared bicycle mobility, (2) the introduction of an ever-widening range of cargo bikes to fit a range of needs and users, and (3) the demand for a better way to travel in our cities during the pandemic. Bike-sharing systems have been around since the 1960s in one form or another, and the first cargo bikes can be traced to the start of the nineteenth century. But the most recent development in cycling, the widespread introduction of the electric-assist motor, has revolutionized cycling as we know it.

I started this book a year after arriving in Oslo, Norway. Mid-pandemic, my family and I sold most of our possessions and moved from our midwestern home in Lincoln, Nebraska, to the Norwegian capital. We were excited about our new adventure—a new language and culture, a new country known for natural beauty and a commitment to sustainability. The process has not been easy, but it has been rewarding. As someone who has devoted his career to sustainable urbanism, it has given me hope for our future as a species to see how much progress Oslo (alongside so many other European cities) has made in a few short years. But by far the most surprising aspect of this adventure has been the clarity with which I can look back across the Atlantic and see the possibilities for the future of American cities.

The urban future we need is one in which cities are dynamic and vibrant environments, with convenient access to everything we need, close enough to reach by bike. What might surprise readers is that this future will be less bike centric than we think. Not everyone needs to ride a bike today or in the future, but bikes are a crucial first step to making car-lite living a reality. For example, while Amsterdam might seem like a bicycle utopia, twice as many people walk and take transit to work as ride every day. The success of Amsterdam is that so few people drive, not that so many people ride a bike. The point of bikes is to help us get there. The goal is making cities better with bikes, rather than for bikes.

The bicycle city is a city where bicycles are the catalyst, not the end goal. Making cities better with bikes means decentering bikes from the narrative. Investing in bicycling has immediate effects, like more people bicycling, but that is only the beginning. In the longer term, modest investments in good infrastructure—infrastructure that makes people want to get out of their cars—lead to fundamental changes in the places we live. The changes help to create places that are welcoming to people—vibrant places where people can interact without fear of being run over by cars, where people can spend time, visit friends or make new ones, and support local shops and restaurants. Ideally, these places have housing options and schools nearby. They can in turn be connected to similar places by bike lanes and transit lines.

Not everyone wants to ride a bike, and not everyone is able to ride a bike. Some people might change their mind given the right circumstances, but a significant number of people will likely never choose to ride or be able to ride. This reality is often forgotten (or ignored) in the conversation about bicycles. It is why we need to talk about bicycles as a means and not an end. Fortunately, if done right, investing in bicycles can improve transportation options for everyone.

Accommodating bicycling in a city can make streets safer and more welcoming for all users. By encouraging bicycling, neighborhoods can become denser, more walkable, and more transit friendly. Planning cities at the scale

Øvre Slottsgate, a car-lite street in central Oslo, Norway. It is one of many changed streets resulting from the city's Car-Free Livability Program. (Credit: Terje Elvsaas)

of the bicycle has the exact opposite effect of making cities around cars. To do this, we need to bring bicycles into the mainstream of transportation. Promoting bicycling in the United States has not been very effective because we do not consider it real transportation. This is largely because historically the practicalities of bicycles have been obscured. Bicycles are treated like toys and not tools by our transportation system. In this way, the very real fun of riding a bike (in addition to its practical benefits) becomes a means to discount its benefits for riders and for cities.

In the United States, there has been very little headway in getting people out of cars, and where there has been progress, it has not been equitable. Walkable and bikeable places are often the least affordable. They are also frequently arrived at through gentrification, creating a damaging link between bicycle infrastructure and displacement. The pattern is this: as wealthy, young White gentrifiers move from the suburbs into urban neighborhoods, bike lanes are seen as a "rolling signifier"[1] of historical disinvestment and racism, as well as of gentrification and displacement of working-class communities and communities of color. While recent research suggests that bike infrastructure tends to come after gentrification and displacement[2] (rather than paving the way for it), bike and pedestrian infrastructure still tends to be the first thing local officials want to talk about (and avoid topics like clean drinking water, overpolicing, or basic accommodations for people with disabilities).

Bicycle urbanism—a loose term for the advocacy movement to foster bicycle-centered cities—has been incredibly successful at reshaping cities to better accommodate biking and walking. But the success of bicycle urbanism, more specifically the way it centers on the *bicycle* part of bicycle urbanism, has made it hard to translate to American cities. There is a far-off, fairy-tale quality to it. The qualitative benefits of the bicycle—the delight that H. G. Wells wrote of—overshadows its quantifiable benefits. The bicycle part of bicycle urbanism becomes the reason it is inapplicable to a big, car-loving country like the United States. It is the result of two cherry-picked narratives, loosely based in history but peppered with myth: the car country narrative and the bicycle urbanism narrative. Revisiting these narratives and looking at them with sober eyes helps us to dispel them.

Car Country

I was a year old when Willie Nelson released "On the Road Again." The song was a fixture on the radio over years of family road trips throughout my childhood. My parents, part of the baby boom generation, grew up in the era of songs like "Little Deuce Coupe" by the Beach Boys (1963) and "Born to Be Wild," performed by Steppenwolf in 1969. This was a time lionized by movies like George Lucas's *American Graffiti* (1973). The songs and movies of the time celebrated the car and all it represented.

We built our cities and lifestyles around cars but, more important, around a dream of what our car-centered life could be: a facade alluding to a dream life, not actually a dream life. In his book *Bicycle Diaries*, David Byrne muses on the aspirational symbolism of modern life. He describes cell phone ringtones as "signs" for "real" music, "music not meant to be actually listened to as music, but to remind you of and refer to other, real, music." He takes this metaphor further, applying it to the suburbs of the cities he visits, characterizing suburbs as "a visual 'description' of a place, but they are not that place." He sees the suburb as a landscape without the heart or soul of a real, lived space, a perfect landscape that "has retained its surface familiarity, virtually, but the deep reasons for its existence—the social and sensual—have been eliminated."[3]

Car culture was birthed in the United States, but culture is not destiny. With the benefit of hindsight, we can see the Pandora's box we opened by investing entirely in car-focused suburban living. The specter of car culture as American identity is a compelling straw man that has successfully blocked most attempts at improving our lives and our communities by reducing auto dependence. People can and do change their behavior all the time. We have the capacity to adapt to changing environments and circumstances. That adaptability is a prerequisite for our continued health and well-being in the face of the climate crisis.

There is growing momentum for reducing car dependence. Generational shifts are demonstrating that the "heartbeat of America" is just a hollow marketing slogan. Millennials, who grew up spending more time being driven to places by their parents than any previous generation, are now driving less than baby boomers or Gen Xers.[4] It's too early to tell whether this trend will continue with Gen Z, but it's a hopeful sign.

The United States today needs a rapid and comprehensive urban transition. We need to move away from fossil fuels and unsustainable lifestyles. We need to transition to sustainable lifestyles in cities that are built around people and not cars—cities that meet the needs of all their residents in sustainable and resilient ways.

The potential is there, but reality is lagging. According to the National Household Travel Survey, currently only about 1 percent of trips nationally are by bike.[5] According to the American Community Survey, 3–6 percent of people commute to work by bike daily in bike-friendly cities like Portland, Minneapolis, or Washington, DC.[6] This pales in comparison with the world's bike capital, Amsterdam, where about 40 percent of people commute by bike.[7] There is an obvious built environment component to this: European cities are, generally, denser than US cities. Most American cities were built around cars, whereas most European cities were built long before the invention of the automobile.

There is reason to hope. In the past few decades, the world has done frighteningly little to address the climate crisis in equitable and effective ways. But freeway removal projects from San Francisco to Seoul and Milwaukee to Madrid have slowly demonstrated the benefits of reorienting our cities toward people. And in the years since the start of the COVID-19 pandemic, ideas such as congestion pricing, "15-minute cities" (the idea that everyone in a city should be able to reach everything they need in a fifteen-minute walk or bike ride), and car-free cities have gone from the fringe to the mainstream.

But the conversation about the future of American cities, and American transportation, trends heavily toward technocratic thinking and could probably use some of the anachronistic humanism associated with the bicycle. The future of mobility focuses narrowly on driverless cars, electrification, and car sharing (i.e., ride hailing). All of these approaches have been roundly criticized as doing nothing more than maintaining an unsustainable, car-centric status quo.[8] In contrast, the future for personal mobility—primarily bikes—offers too many potential benefits to count.

Fifty years after the oil embargo that led the Dutch to embrace bicycles, another crisis, the pandemic, has led to a boom in bicycling and a radical rethinking of the future of urban mobility. The possibility of a car-lite urban future is very real.

Bicycle Urbanism

The undisputed capital of bicycle urbanism is Amsterdam. The idea of the bicycle as urban savior features heavily in the origin story of Amsterdam (and the Netherlands in general) as a bicycle paradise. If you have had the chance to visit Amsterdam, you know that it is both truth and marketing. Amsterdam functions for its residents in so many positive ways because of its reliance on the bicycle as a foundation for moving around the city. If you haven't been to Amsterdam, you have almost definitely seen the pictures, videos, memes, and commentary that are so ubiquitous in the media surrounding bicycle urbanism.

Bicycle urbanism in Amsterdam. (Credit: iStock/lechatnoir)

Despite its truth, sometimes the bicycle urbanism narrative does more harm than good. There's a quasi-religious quality to it that can be divisive (i.e., there are bike people, and there is everyone else) and can obscure two important truths: (1) bicycles make cities better for everyone, not just for cyclists, and (2) bicycles can work anywhere, from cities to small towns, and are not just for Europe's metropolitan elite (whatever that means).

Bicycles have inspired devotion because they really are a great invention with a lot of potential. The devotion followed the utility, but sometimes this fact gets lost. The story of Amsterdam as a bicycle paradise illustrates this point.

The story goes that the bicycle has, since its inception, been central to Dutch culture. In the postwar years of the 1950s, as people watched their streets cede space to cars, they organized and fought back. In response to the growing number of people killed by Dutch motorists (3,000 people were killed in 1971, of whom 450 were children), activists started the Stop de Kindermoord (Stop the Murder of Children) movement, demanding better bicycle infrastructure in Dutch cities.[9] Opposition to the car grew throughout the 1960s, and the 1970s oil crisis pushed the government to act. The Dutch loved their precious bicycles, bikes do not depend on oil, and bike lanes are cheap. At the confluence of culture, organized protest, and the economics of an unprecedented global energy crisis, the bicycle city was born.

As with any story that is told repeatedly, the details blur and the nuance is lost. The root of the aspirational narrative of bicycling may be that the Dutch story is often told backward, confusing correlation with causation. The bicycle holds a special place in Dutch culture, but cultural affinity goes only so far. The Dutch are notoriously direct, analytical, and industrious. The story of a people so in love with a nineteenth-century toy that they rebuilt their cities around it invokes an anachronistic charm that can feel especially appealing in today's increasingly technocratic world but has little basis in reality.

Almost next door to the Dutch (the Netherlands and Denmark don't share a border), the Danes came to similar conclusions about bicycles. Their capital, Copenhagen, has more than kept pace with Amsterdam as a world leader in bicycle urbanism. But there's no historical evidence of any particular love of the bicycle in Danish culture. Copenhagen's tourism website states: "What is it about Copenhageners that makes them take to the bicycle every morning come rain, sleet, or snow? Is the average Copenhagener more eco-conscious than you? Hardly. Is it because they're all a bunch of health freaks? Not a chance. Or maybe because the bicycle is just part of the Danish DNA? Nope. It comes down to three important factors: Infrastructure, infrastructure, and infrastructure."[10]

Despite the world-renowned bicycle pedigree the Dutch are so well known for, the myriad similarities between Denmark and the Netherlands help to create an imperfect natural experiment: when controlled for as many other factors as possible, "bike culture" does not appear significant in jump-starting an urban transition away from the car.

The Dutch and the Danes realized the benefits of bicycles for everyone, not just people on bikes. While they have spent the past fifty years realizing those benefits and refining their unique versions of bicycle urbanism, the United States has continued to obsessively pave more miles of highways. The results of these distinct paths are clear. Bikes support vibrant places and livable streets; cars do not. Bicycle urbanism supports compact and sustainable cities, while auto dependence precludes sustainability. Bicycle urbanism fosters the kinds of places that require less infrastructure to support and maintain, the kinds of places that encourage community and build social capital. Bicycles are cheap, convenient, and useful. They are safe and efficient and do not inhibit other uses of public streets. Bike infrastructure costs almost nothing compared with wide roads and parking lots, but also compared with public transit.

The benefits of bicycles were also self-evident on the other side of the world, to the Communist government of the People's Republic of China. During the post–World War II era, China was sometimes called a "bicycle kingdom" thanks to the millions of Flying Pigeon bicycles produced and ridden daily over the course of about forty years from 1950 to 1990. The benefits of the bicycle as a cheap and flexible transport mode were clear to a rapidly industrializing country that didn't have money to spend on public transit. Unfortunately, starting in the 1990s, cars began to replace bicycles. Driving became associated with progress.[11] By 2010, more cars were sold in China than in any other country.[12] In 2022, 33 percent of car sales worldwide were in China.[13]

In the late 1960s and early 1970s, Amsterdam and Copenhagen were on similar trajectories toward auto dependence, but a global energy crisis galvanized support for a dramatic course correction in urban development. Looking at the intervening decades, we can trace the urban development trajectories of the Dutch and the Danes and see how they resulted in very different outcomes from that in the United States. Rather than an urban transformation in support of cities for cars, these two nations used the bicycle to transition toward what the Danish architect and designer Jan Gehl calls human-scaled cities.

What happened to the United States? We were not immune to the effects of the 1970s oil crisis, but it inspired a push toward fuel efficiency and a reliance on domestic oil rather than a rethinking of auto dependence. In the intervening decades, we have done little to course correct away from auto dominance, with the exception of some efforts by larger, progressive cities. Because of this piecemeal approach to bicycle urbanism, these efforts resulted in high-priced islands of walkable and bikeable places in seas of suburban auto dependence.[14]

Path dependence helps to explain America's auto addiction: the sheer momentum of a country as big as the United States and an economic and political engine myopically focused on creating the auto age. The auto age began at the start of the twentieth century, and we have not meaningfully strayed from a path of car-centric development since.

The creation and maintenance of auto dependence in the United States is a lot like the massive container ships that maintain global supply chains. These ships, which can weigh a quarter of a million tons when loaded with thousands of containers, are incapable of doing anything quickly. They require hours and miles to speed up, slow down, or turn. Getting something this massive to deviate from its current course and trajectory is not easy.

That's not to say it's impossible to course correct. But the work of reducing auto dependence in US cities is slow going. It is early days yet in the United States' effort to pivot toward human-centered living. Efforts to promote or encourage bicycling often feel like Band-Aids or consolation prizes in American cities or tokens to appease frustrated bike advocates while still maintaining the auto-oriented status quo. Because of this, most Americans have never seen or experienced the very real benefits of bicycles, to individuals or to the community. Or, if they have, they have seen it only in marketing materials to encourage Amsterdam tourism, not viable strategies to improve their own hometowns.

Unlike the Dutch and the Danes, Americans have not put any real effort into using the bicycle as a viable means of transportation. In the 1960s and 1970s, the baby boom kids who grew up riding Schwinn bicycles—heavy, straight-gauge steel behemoths welded by World War II veterans in factories in the Midwest—came of age and were inspired by the environmental movement to change their lifestyle. The bicycle became central to a cleaner, greener way of life.

But larger forces—market forces and policies and planning favoring the car—prevailed. Just as the hippie environmentalism of the 1970s became a caricature of itself, so did the bicycle. To be a cyclist meant embodying all the negative stereotypes of the anachronistic hippie: a child of privilege who had turned on, tuned in, and dropped out, hugging trees and getting high while the rest of world continued on with the serious business of reality. The bicycle was no longer just a bicycle but a constellation of symbolic identities, including privileged Whiteness, radical environmentalism, and a general incompatibility with modern society. These associations continue to plague bicycle advocacy today and can explain why, for example, national policies for electrifying vehicles can proceed apace while national-level support for electric bicycles languishes, despite the fact that e-bikes are outselling electric vehicles by a wide margin.[15]

Electronic bikes—e-bikes—are simple. Just take a standard bicycle and add a small electric motor and rechargeable battery pack. The crucial difference between an e-bike and a motorcycle or moped is that the e-bike motor engages only when the rider pedals. This distinction has been codified into state legislation in much of the country and was developed to distinguish e-bikes from other forms of motorized transport, such as motorcycles and mopeds, and to provide some clarity for US bicycle manufacturers.

E-assist technology has been integrated into all types of bicycles and increasingly into bikeshare systems. E-assist is available on high-end mountain and road bikes for the spandex crowd. It is especially popular among older people who want to stay active but appreciate the assistance and couples where one person may need the e-assist to keep pace.

But the real explosion in e-bikes has been among commuters, delivery riders, older people, people with disabilities, and others who may not immediately identify as cyclists. It is helped by an expanding range of electric cargo bicycles that can cater to all types of people and needs. Cargo bikes, until recently a niche product, at least in the United States, are suddenly growing in popularity across the country thanks to electric-assist motors. With e-assist, cargo bikes are being adapted for urban freight delivery, family transportation, and a growing range of specialized needs. E-bicycles and e-cargo bikes can meet more needs for more people than standard bicycles ever could. It is a simple innovation that is changing the game.

The Pandemic Bike Boom

We may never know the human cost of the coronavirus pandemic, but there are some important lessons for cities and urban transport that we cannot ignore. The first is that more people than ever before got out on their bikes when they were stuck at home. The second lesson of the pandemic is that things can change fast—almost unbelievably so. The pandemic bike boom was simultaneously shocking and obvious. While it can be difficult to separate hopes from facts, the lesson is that we have agency to manifest the things we require from our cities.

There's a bad joke in the bike industry (and probably in a dozen other industries): How do you make a little money from a bike shop? Start with a lot. But in the bike industry's case, the pandemic changed everything. Almost immediately after the pandemic began, bike shops were suddenly busy. Surprising everyone, especially those in the bike world, bike shops were busier than they had ever been. It wasn't only shops: the bike industry—from frame builders to parts manufacturers—couldn't keep pace with demand, and that trend continued for at least two years.[16]

The demand for bicycles coincided with a demand for public space tailored to people. Politicians and planners took notice. People needed places to gather while also mitigating the spread of an airborne virus—that is, outdoor spaces. Between parking lots and wide streets, American cities have a lot of underutilized space between buildings. Suddenly, the types of changes for which so many of us have been advocating for years, retaking streets from cars and giving them back to the people who live on them, was not just possible but actually happening.

Almost overnight in March 2020, traffic disappeared from streets and highways. Some people switched to remote work, others lost their jobs, and still others continued to go to work in person. I physically shudder every time I hear the term "new normal," but we all were suddenly, rapidly, confronted with exactly that.

As the initial shock of the pandemic faded and our understanding of the coronavirus evolved, people began coming out into the streets and seeing potential where they once saw only traffic, realizing that being stuck at home didn't have to mean stuck inside. Without a daily commute, people had additional hours per day at their disposal. One study found a 16 percent increase in bicycling in the United States from 2019 to 2020, with most of that additional riding done on weekends.[17] For bike mechanics who worked through the early days of the pandemic, it seemed as if every bicycle in every garage and basement in the United States rolled through their shop for the first tune-up in years (or ever).

Nationally and globally, urban spaces were reinvigorated. Approximately two hundred US cities changed their streets—for example, by instituting traffic calming and closing car lanes—in an effort to support increased bicycling in their communities.[18] The presence of people and the (relative) absence of cars fundamentally changes a place. Research demonstrates that these places become safer from car crashes and create a positive feedback loop in which the presence of people begets more of the same.[19] And businesses and politicians followed. Street closures for outdoor events, food trucks, and outdoor cafés all contributed to an increasingly bold experiment in urbanism.

But the pandemic bike boom is about more than bicycling; it is about urban resilience—the ability to withstand or recover quickly from shocks. The bicycle just happens to feature prominently as a side effect, a release valve for some of the pressures the pandemic placed on people and places. What happened with bicycling is also a proof of concept for what so many urbanists have been advocating for decades: cities for people.[20]

Deus ex Machina

I started this chapter with a quote from H. G. Wells: "Every time I see an adult on a bicycle, I no longer despair for the future of the human race." I have a complicated relationship with this quote. I find it both inspirational and sanctimonious. On the one hand, it offers hope to the faithful that the bicycle is the answer to all our problems—the simple solution to a complex problem. On the other, it leaves no room for those who are not sold on the dream of bicycle utopia.

I am not saying that riding a bike isn't fun. I count myself as a cyclist, and I have experienced the exhilaration and freedom, the newness of places experienced by bike. But the *whole bike thing* can be exclusionary, sexist, ableist, expensive, and exhausting to a lot of people, negating any potential value of a bicycle for helping to create better, more sustainable, and more inclusive cities.

I advocate for using the bicycle to enable rapid but incremental changes that, to paraphrase the most common definition of sustainability, improve the conditions of the present while also improving conditions for future generations.[21] That means meeting everyone's needs, not only the needs of those who currently ride a bike or those who could be convinced to do so. Meeting everyone's needs requires thinking beyond bicycle cities and simply striving for high-quality places where cars are unnecessary for most people most of the time. In such places, bicycling is safe and convenient but also transit is clean, efficient, and dependable, and those who do need to use a car, such as people with disabilities, have the ability to do so. High-quality places that meet everyone's needs combine form and function—urban density that is not oppressive, convenient access to destinations, and a range of options for getting there.

This combination of form and function, at a price a normal person can afford, is vanishingly rare in the United States.[22] The challenge is to move from automobile dependence to higher and better uses of our shared urban spaces. Bicycles can get us there. We don't need to wait for Silicon Valley to figure out autonomous vehicle technology. We don't all need to buy electric cars, and we don't need to build a new national grid to charge them. Bicycles are here, and they are proven. I am hopeful that it is not too late.

Almost everyone is familiar with the story of the frog in the pot. As the story goes, if a frog is placed in boiling water it will jump out, but if it is put in tepid water and the temperature is raised slowly, it won't notice and will boil to death. It has become the go-to metaphor for humanity's response, or lack thereof, to global warming. Al Gore used it in his 2006 documentary *An Inconvenient Truth* (in Gore's version, the frog was rescued before it could be harmed). The assumption is that climate change takes place too gradually for us to grasp its severity,[23] and therefore we neglect to act until it is too late.

But the climate is changing fast enough for us all to see. Every year and every decade, we are experiencing new weather extremes and breaking global temperature predictions. The 1990s were the hottest decade on record, then the 2000s, and then the 2010s. Every summer brings new variations of the phrase "This is the hottest summer so far and the coolest summer of the rest of our lives."[24] The most recent report of the Intergovernmental Panel on Climate Change (as of this writing) warns that the window for mitigating the most dire consequences of climate change—by limiting global warming to 1.5°C (2.7°F)—is narrowing.[25]

It's easy (for me, at least) to panic or become paralyzed by the apparent inevitability of global warming, but the reality is that there is no such thing as too late. It is definitely too late for our current climate—the one we know, can trace historically, and understand. Jeff Goodell, author of the book *The Heat Will Kill You First: Life and Death on a Scorched Planet*, makes the point that people tend to assume we can reverse the changes we have caused to our planet, but that is "a profound misunderstanding of the moment that we're in. . . . We are moving into a different world, and we need to grasp that idea."[26]

Goodell likens current thinking about the climate crisis to the American experience with the Clean Air Act, which was extremely effective at reducing air pollution (and its associated health and environmental consequences).[27] Because of the success of efforts such as the Clean Air Act, we tend to think of climate change as reversible. But the nature of the problem is different. Smog and particulate matter—the primary targets of the Clean Air Act—were comparatively simple to clean up and had few lasting consequences for the planet. As Goodell points out, carbon dioxide "is essentially permanent when we put it up there. . . . And the warming will not stop until we stop emitting CO_2 and burning fossil fuels. . . . And even if we stop CO_2, we are stuck with that warming planet for a very long time."[28]

The frog hasn't boiled. Leaving behind the climate of the past and entering an unknown new climate reality is not a reason to give up. Cities have the potential to address the short-term uncertainties of a new climate that will be hotter and less predictable. And if done correctly, those same adaptations can become the long-term solution to stopping emissions and in turn stopping further warming. An urban climate solution is, in turn, a global climate solution.

According to the United Nations Environment Programme, cities are responsible for about 75 percent of global emissions and are home to more than half of Earth's population.[29] The solution starts with changing how we travel and ends with changing our cities. And the bicycle (with or without electronic assistance) is the key to this plan. People need alternatives to the car. Many cities lack the money or political will to invest in transit, but bicycling is cheap and can use existing infrastructure. Development can change to serve people on bikes; such development is denser and can encourage walking. Urban density is more efficient and sustainable; that is, more people can be served by less infrastructure. Denser places are more resilient because there is less physical space that needs to be maintained and potentially protected from extreme weather. Finally, the additional transportation options associated with denser places mean more flexibility in the case of evacuation, as opposed to having everyone with a car stuck in traffic and everyone without a car stuck in the path of danger.

Cities for Everyone

An effective urban transition starts with people and ends with places. It is easy to lose sight of the fact that we all have had a hand, directly or indirectly, in shaping our cities. Most people don't think about the systems in place in our cities that have created haves and have-nots. The transportation system plays an integral part in feeding an unsustainable and unjust system.

Housing policies that placed the American dream of a house with a yard within reach of so many depended on federal transportation spending on roads and highways to connect cities and suburbs. These same systems—the combination of transportation and development policies and programs—have for generations led to systematic disinvestment in and devastation of marginalized communities and communities of color. The systems that spurred homeownership and intergenerational wealth have resulted in the wealth of White families being ten times that of Black families.[30]

The Black Lives Matter movement has drawn national attention back to inequities in American society. As with the civil rights movement a generation earlier, Black Lives Matter protests were frequently held on roads and highways, blocking traffic as a means to be heard. The streets and freeways employed as a stage for protest also highlight the discriminatory practices, and violent outcomes, that characterize policing in the United States. A 2020 study published in *Nature Human Behaviour* examined racial disparities in traffic stops across the United States and found that Black and Hispanic drivers were stopped and searched more often than White drivers.[31] Furthermore, in 2022, police were more likely to harm or kill people of color in traffic stops, including stops for minor infractions.[32]

Transportation policy rarely addresses the role of automobile dependence in perpetuating violence against people of color, but it is essential that as we transition away from auto dependence, we do not repeat past mistakes. Advocates for healthy and livable cities often cite equity goals alongside sustainability goals—a racial justice version of greenwashing. Bicycle advocacy and promotion, in turn, has a well-documented history of equity and inclusion problems. To be absolutely clear, the bicycle, electric, shared, or otherwise, is not a panacea for society's problems. At its best, the bicycle is a catalyst.

We cannot address the climate crisis in a truly sustainable way without simultaneously addressing the role of transportation in systemic racism, segregation, and gentrification. Doing so via mobility transitions is an indirect and modest solution at best, further social justice greenwashing at worst. But using every tool we have at our disposal to address the immediate inequities in our society is a start. I use the pronoun "we" here purposely because this is not a process that can done without everyone in the room.

Something as simple and utilitarian as an e-bike, when put in the hands of those who need it (via incentives, grants, tax breaks, or shared services), can be a viable car replacement at a fraction of the cost. Flexible housing and zoning programs—the kinds that increase access to homeownership for those who cannot qualify for traditional mortgages—are made more viable without parking requirements. And reducing automobile ownership means not only more space on roads but also more empty garages that can be converted into living spaces, which can be rented out for supplemental income or used by extended family to foster intergenerational living.

This may sound naïve, but it is all well within the realm of possibility. Equitable and flexible housing policies depend on our fundamentally altering our relationship with the car. Reducing city space devoted to cars (and parking)[33] is essential. Momentum for this is growing in the United States and internationally, but people still need to get around quickly and efficiently. They need to be able to travel with family members and with their stuff. Improving public transit is essential to this, as is retrofitting our communities to have more destinations closer.

The first step is to put a viable car replacement within reach of a majority of Americans. Once that is done, we can work our way toward the real goals of car-lite urbanism. Getting from here (auto dependence) to there (a car-lite urban future) will look different in every community. Creating sustainable, equitable, and livable cities means rethinking transportation as connected to all of the current problems in our cities but also as a key to unlocking the potential of our cities, and quickly.

The challenges and opportunities for our cities span infrastructure, policy, and human behavior. They require us to better utilize the land and resources we have while preserving natural resources, all in sustainable and equitable ways. According to the authors of the Intergovernmental Panel on Climate Change's 2022 report, the path forward for a shared human future can be realized "by involving everyone in planning, attention to equity and justice, and drawing on Indigenous and local knowledge."[34]

We have struggled in the United States to best utilize the tools we have at our disposal to address our most pressing societal problems. In the case of the bicycle, we have been hobbled by the path dependence of a century of auto-oriented planning—a century that has enshrined unhealthy, inequitable, and unsustainable urbanism in our daily lives and the shape of our cities. The introduction of e-bikes has changed the game in bicycle urbanism, broadening the base of support and enthusiasm for changing the way we get around. In light of new technologies, options, and opportunities, we can reenvision the bicycle as a catalyst for urban change. We can harness the post-pandemic bike boom, and the emergence of electric bikes and cargo bikes, to push an urban transition to a future that is not about making cities better *for* bikes but making cities better *with* bikes.

1

The Pandemic and the Bicycle Boom

CITIES WERE HIT FIRST AND HARDEST by the initial waves of the COVID-19 pandemic in 2020. Buses stopped running; stores, schools, and offices closed. In New York City, those living near hospitals witnessed in shocking disbelief the arrival of temporary morgues—refrigerated trailers parked outside hospitals, called body collection points by emergency planners.[1]

In what felt like a doomsday situation, lockdowns emptied the streets. The only people going out were medical professionals, service workers, or those with the means to flee the city. The *New York Times* asked, "Can City Life Survive Coronavirus?," in an article posted on March 17, 2020.[2] Anti-urbanism has a long history in the United States, a result of historical perceptions of cities as corrupt and unhealthy, wrapped up in racism and anti-immigrant stereotypes.[3] Unfortunately, in the early days of the pandemic, the picture of a post-coronavirus world was forming as a by-product of fear and confusion, and the image was grim.

Despite having been ranked number one in pandemic preparedness by the World Health Organization before the pandemic, the United States failed across all metrics to control the spread of COVID-19.[4] The US death toll caused by the virus is shocking, estimated by the Centers for Disease Control and Prevention at over one million people as of 2023,[5] and statistics likely underreport the actual number. Those deaths were primarily among the most vulnerable: those with underlying conditions and poor access to health care.

The pandemic acted as an accelerant, lighter fuel on the myriad already smoldering slow-motion crises in our cities. The tensions boiled over onto streets and into the public realm. Transportation featured prominently in these crises, from a bus driver becoming the victim of an anti-mask attack to anti-Asian violence on city streets and the persistent murders of Black Americans by police during routine traffic stops. Talking about the pandemic in the singular obfuscates the extent of the inequities in its impacts.

COVID-19 disproportionately affected marginalized racial groups, those with less income and wealth, and immigrants. In their interactive COVID-19 Health Inequities in Big Cities Health Coalition (BCHC) Dashboard, researchers at Drexel University documented how Black, Latino, and Native American persons faced a constellation of increased risks during the pandemic, including overrepresentation in high-risk occupations and increased likelihood of living in crowded conditions in underserved areas.[6]

In the wake of so much injustice and tragedy, it can feel dismissive to spotlight the lessons from the increase in biking during the pandemic, and that is not my goal. The bike narrative presented only as a simple, feel-good story of people rediscovering their love of cycling while working from home undercuts the significance of what happened and what it means for cities. My goal is to contextualize the increase in bicycling and draw lessons from the pandemic for making our cities better—more just, more sustainable, and more livable.

The pandemic is certainly not over, but it is already clear that it did not signal the death of cities. As the world adapts to living with COVID-19, we can create a clearer picture of what the pandemic has meant for cities.

Stanford University economist Paul Romer said in 2004 that "a crisis is a terrible thing to waste,"[7] and amid the tragedy, the pandemic holds lessons for improving our cities. As people sought safe ways to socialize and be active, and cities sought ways to support businesses, rates of walking and bicycling began to climb[8] and streets began to change. So-called pandemic street experiments, often temporary changes to streets that occasionally became permanent, began appearing across the United States. For example, New York City created Open Streets and Open Restaurants programs that gave pedestrians and bicycles priority on some streets and allowed restaurants to use street space for outdoor dining.[9] In California, Berkeley implemented a Healthy Streets program, and Oakland implemented a Slow Streets program—both of which aimed to reduce traffic on residential streets.[10]

Collectively, increases in cycling and efforts by cities to support them are referred to as the pandemic bike boom. Many of those stuck at home, either working remotely or having lost their job because of the pandemic, dusted off their old bicycles (or bought new ones) so they could get outside to exercise, enjoy some fresh air, and socialize while maintaining social distancing.[11] For those who relied on transit and had to continue working in person, bicycles offered a cheap and healthy alternative.[12] Of course, commutes for some people, such as service workers and medical workers, remained unchanged. But with the influx of people on bikes, some cities responded to the needs of new cyclists seeking safe places to ride and businesses seeking ways to stay afloat by experimenting with street spaces now largely devoid of traffic. A survey

Temporary pandemic street experiment in Seattle, Washington. (Credit: SDOT)

of 200 US cities found that about half of them (102 cities) built new bike infrastructure, 72 percent closed streets to cars (creating "open streets"), and 35 percent reduced motor vehicle speed limits.[13]

Improvements to bicycle and pedestrian infrastructure offered a glimpse of how our cities could be, but the future is uncertain. It is not clear what will remain of the actual infrastructure or the political will that made it happen. Of the programs I mentioned that began during the pandemic, New York's Open Streets and Open Restaurants programs remain, but Berkeley's Healthy Streets does not.[14] Oakland's Slow Streets program initially ended after a year, but it was reinstated by popular demand.[15] At the same time, remote work is now an expectation for many, and that has translated to empty downtown offices and packed neighborhood coffee shops. Our cities are functioning differently now. The ebb and flow of movement, the journeys and destinations, and the way these shift throughout the day has changed for so many of us, potentially permanently.

The Pandemic Effect

On March 11, 2020, the World Health Organization officially declared a global pandemic. A day later, most college and professional sports leagues suspended their seasons. A day after that, on Friday, March 13, the United States declared a national emergency[16] and states began implementing an array of shutdown measures aimed at controlling the spread of the virus.

Shutdowns meant that most people didn't go to work or school, and that was reflected on streets and highways. Nationally, traffic dropped by almost 65 percent. Depending on the state, traffic volumes dropped by 40–65 percent at the start of the pandemic.[17] Traffic engineers were stunned. Traffic reductions such as these were unprecedented. They happened basically overnight, as the result of a sweeping policy decision. Nothing new was built. No new lanes were added. It was an important moment of recognition that *we* create traffic, in the ways we structure workdays and locate workplaces far from our homes, requiring cars to get there. Automobile infrastructure in turn destroys and isolates neighborhoods, contributes to food deserts, and increases air pollution and heat island effects. We can thus adjust the settings in such a way as to eliminate traffic and mitigate its consequences.

The standard toolbox for dealing with traffic congestion includes building new roads, widening roads, implementing tolls, and optimizing traffic signals. All of these take time and money. Because of induced demand,[18] these tools actually worsen congestion in the long run. They fail because they are based on a narrow understanding of the causal mechanisms behind the amount, the supply, of traffic on our roads. They are based on the assumption that there will always be traffic because there will always be a need, a demand, to travel. Historically, traffic engineers have always assumed that the demand and the corresponding amounts of traffic will grow. Pandemic shutdowns forced a reevaluation of the assumptions underlying traffic, namely, what if no one needs to go anywhere?

For those lucky people who were able to work remotely and remain safe at home, the pandemic initiated a reevaluation of daily activities and travel.[19] Some people realized that the act of commuting, particularly by bike, had qualitative benefits beyond simply getting to work. In its absence, "fake bike commutes"[20] gained popularity, becoming a coping mechanism for some. For others, simply going for a bike ride, without calling it anything else, helped to mitigate the stress of the pandemic. Nationally, bicycling increased by an estimated 16 percent from 2019 to 2020.[21] New York's Department of Transportation reported a 50 percent increase in bicycle traffic, and Philadelphia reported an increase of 150 percent.[22]

The data suggest that most of the pandemic bike boom can be attributed to increased recreational riding, that is, riding without a clear destination and therefore riding for a purpose other than *getting somewhere*. This is in contrast to commuting or utilitarian travel, in which there is a clear destination that implies a reason for leaving the house. When broken down into weekday versus weekend travel, there was a 10 percent increase in bicycling on weekdays but a 29 percent increase on weekends (a similar pattern was found in European data). Additionally, bicycling increased on recreational trails and in the afternoon and evening hours. The number of cyclists dropped on streets and in commercial areas and during typical commute times.[23]

It's easy to dismiss the significance of recreational riding, but that is a mistake. We value utility, efficiency, and productivity in transportation systems, and therefore anything recreational is by definition antithetical to those values. The fact that the pandemic bike boom was largely measured in terms of recreational activity is an artifact of circumstance. We count bicycle traffic as one or the other, when what is important is the total amount of traffic. The raw numbers, regardless of why a person is riding, give an idea of how many people could be riding on our streets and in our cities. These could be people commuting to work, picking up groceries, getting some exercise, or meeting friends at a coffee shop, given the right circumstances. Vibrant and human-scaled urbanism does not depend on why people are out of their cars, but it does depend on how many people are.

Whatever that total number is serves as a baseline for latent demand for riding—the potential for bicycling right now. That baseline potential tells communities that if they provide the right circumstances (mostly remove the fear of being hit by cars), a significant number of people will be willing and able to get out on two wheels. That is what the so-called recreational riding numbers recorded during the pandemic provide, and it is why they shouldn't be dismissed as *just* recreational trips. It is an imperfect measure, but it's the best measure we have. That increase in riding offers a glimpse at an alternative reality. We arrived at this view from global tragedy, but it is a critical data point for understanding the speed and extent of change that is possible.

Traffic

"When a situation feels dangerous to you, it's probably more safe than you know; when a situation feels safe, that is precisely when you should feel on guard." Tom Vanderbilt wrote this about traffic safety. In his 2009 book *Traffic: Why We Drive the Way We Do (and What It Says about Us)*, he tells the story of how Sweden switched from driving on the left to driving on the right, to bring driving practice in line with that of neighboring countries. After a year of preparation, planning, and outreach, in the early morning of Sunday, September 3, 1967, Sweden made the switch. Despite fears of an increase in crashes, crash rates dropped dramatically and did not rise to pre-switch levels for two years. The improved safety is widely attributed to the fact that people felt unsafe and thus drove more carefully.

This effect, this glitch of human cognition, explains why places with more cycling and walking are safer and why a higher number of bicycles passing through an intersection improves safety for everyone crossing that intersection: when there is a lot going on, drivers need to be more aware, and that results in safer places.

Unfortunately, the opposite is also true. As Vanderbilt goes on to say, "Most crashes, after all, happen on dry roads, on clear, sunny days, to sober drivers." This is exactly what happened during the pandemic. According to the US Department of Transportation's National Highway Traffic Safety Administration, in the first half of 2021 traffic fatalities increased by nearly 20 percent,[24] resulting from the few remaining drivers, taking advantage of empty roads, driving more dangerously and paying less attention.[25]

In the United States, we use laws and enforcement to try to make our roads safer. The rationale is that if people are scared of penalties (like tickets, fines, and possibly prison time), they will drive more safely. While enforcement plays a part in any approach to traffic safety, it cannot be the primary approach. But in the United States, we do just that. We design our streets to move as many vehicles as possible as quickly as possible. Safety is secondary in the design process. We instead focus on traffic laws and enforcement to ensure road safety. This approach is misguided and ineffective. All available evidence demonstrates that it serves only to exacerbate racist overpolicing.[26]

The most effective solution for road safety is to take a systems approach to the problem: that is, change the system to lessen the likelihood and severity of crashes. The traditional approach to road safety, through enforcement, assumes that people can be trained to behave in safer ways. Instead, a systems approach recognizes that people inevitably make mistakes, but we can redesign our transportation system to anticipate those mistakes. In turn, we can lessen their likelihood and severity through better street design and infrastructure, safer vehicles, and policies. Promoting safety through design is much more effective than enforcing traffic rules.[27] This forms the backbone of the Vision Zero movement (the movement to reduce traffic deaths to zero), which started in Sweden in the 1990s. Whereas Vision Zero is orthodoxy in Scandinavia, and has been for decades, it has struggled to gain traction in the United States,[28] where we design for speed and not safety. Crashes are a feature, not a bug. Because we expect crashes, we design roads in a forgiving way. The goal is to limit the damage from a crash, not reduce the possibility of a crash.

When it comes to mobilizing policy to effect change, another part of the problem is that a systems perspective of traffic safety is a relatively abstract concept. It is difficult to explain without context but easy to understand when experienced firsthand. Prior to the pandemic, most people had very little time to take a walk or go for a ride in their neighborhood, either alone or with their families. Pandemic shutdowns forced this experience on millions of Americans.

The pandemic bike boom brought about a massive role reversal on US streets. Rather than being the driver speeding through the neighborhood to get to work, people suddenly became the walker or person on a bike, many for the first time. It's a nerve-racking experience. When a six-thousand-pound sport utility vehicle passes within a few feet of someone on a bike, it's a minor inconvenience for the driver. But for the cyclist, it's a visceral experience: it is loud, it is shocking, and the force of the air pressure alone can shake even experienced cyclists. It can be terrifying if you're new to cycling and even more terrifying if you are looking out for your kids as well.

Instead of being annoyed with bicyclists, bike lanes, and crosswalks as a driver, when walking or bicycling for the first time, many Americans found themselves wishing for more of these exact types of basic accommodations. The pandemic jump-started a conversation, owing largely to a public demanding that leaders do better to provide safe and welcoming public places. That meant utilizing the newly cleared streets and parking lots in cities under some version of pandemic shutdown.

I doubt many people out riding a bike for the first time thought much about how we tend to characterize cyclists in the United States. In movies, characters who ride bikes generally fall into one of three categories: the oddball, the athlete, or the scofflaw. A string of movies from the 1970s and 1980s illustrate the types. Pee-wee Herman in *Pee-wee's Big Adventure* (1985) is probably the best example of the weirdo. *Breaking Away* (1979) and *American Flyers* (1985) showcase the athlete. And Kevin Bacon's starring role as a bike messenger in *Quicksilver* (1986) showcases the scofflaw stereotype.

The stereotype endures; for example, Steve Carell's portrayal of the titular character in *The 40-Year-Old Virgin* (2005) and Mark Wahlberg's performance in *I Heart Huckabees* (2004) are more recent examples of the oddball.

The (animated) *Triplets of Belleville* (2003) satirizes the athlete, while *Premium Rush* (2012) updates the scofflaw stereotype. The commonality among them all is that they are all weird. They are out of step with normal people and normal society.

The Scofflaw Cyclist

Scofflaw cyclists are careless, unpredictable, and dangerous. They ride wherever they want, whenever they want, ignoring traffic laws and other road users. The scofflaw cyclist is a lawless, pedal-powered speed demon set on terrorizing good, wholesome, and honest drivers everywhere. The scofflaw cyclist stereotype is invoked anytime a bike project is proposed in a city. The logic from the anti-bike crowd is that investing in bicycling is using public funds to support these crazies.

Everyone breaks traffic laws, usually minor ones, and usually without consequence. Almost everyone has jaywalked or driven slightly over the speed limit. These behaviors are technically illegal but are generally considered acceptable. But when bicyclists break traffic laws, it's a different story. The vitriol and anger, mostly from drivers, is extreme. Before the pandemic, some colleagues and I sought to understand the rage aimed at cyclists who break minor traffic laws. Our hope was that we could understand the roots of the rage against scofflaw cyclists, to break down barriers to investing in cycling in our cities.

We created an online survey to ask people about how they rode. We asked people how much they walked, rode, or drove, how many (and what kinds of) laws they broke, and why they did so. We also included a series of hypothetical scenarios, with pictures and descriptions of different scenarios.

When analyzing the data, we first looked at lawbreaking in general and found that everyone is a criminal: 100 percent of those who took the survey reported breaking traffic laws, whether riding a bike, walking, or driving a car. In the hypothetical situations we presented in the survey, 95.87 percent of bicyclists, 97.90 percent of pedestrians, and nearly all drivers (99.97 percent) selected responses that would be considered illegal.[29]

We weren't all that surprised to find that everyone breaks minor traffic laws, but what surprised us was why: the reasons varied according to whether someone was walking, riding a bike, or driving a car. When cycling, the most common reason for doing something illegal was a concern for *personal safety*. The next most common reasons were *saving energy*, followed by *saving time*. In contrast to why people broke laws when cycling, the most popular reason for lawbreaking when driving and walking was to save time (i.e., speeding and jaywalking). This makes sense if you have ever tried to ride a bike in the United States. Our cities lack good bicycle infrastructure, so cyclists have to do their best while navigating systems that were not designed to accommodate them. This could mean running a red light to get ahead of cars or riding on the sidewalk to avoid interacting with cars entirely.

Cyclists weren't breaking traffic laws any more than anyone else, but they did so because they were scared.

Next, we looked at what contributes to drivers getting so angry at scofflaw cyclists, asking people to explain why. Some people were angry at scofflaw cyclists out of a sense of injustice; for example, one commenter wrote, "If they want to use the roads, they need to obey the highway rules EXACTLY the same as anyone driving" (emphasis his). But others were angry because they thought that scofflaws were making other cyclists look bad. One person commented that "it hurts biking in general." Others got mad at scofflaw cyclists because they didn't behave in the way the driver expected them to; that is, they didn't break laws properly. One person wrote, "If it (lawbreaking) is done with some sense and reasoning and not for the sake of not obeying I am fine with it."[30]

But reasonable lawbreaking is totally subjective. In the words of another commenter regarding scofflaw cyclists, "Don't be an asshole and we'll do just fine." This comment in turn suggests the underlying power imbalance on roads. If a driver wants to enforce their idea of appropriate behavior, they have a few thousand pounds of steel to do so. This theme came up a lot in our survey, with people writing things like "They think they are above the law" and "It's like they dare you to hit them."

What we learned was that bicyclists are stuck in a no-win situation on our roads. Without infrastructure in place to dictate appropriate behavior or to separate traffic and bicyclists, bicyclists are at the mercy of drivers. It is a common problem on streets.[31] If you have lived in the Northeast, you may be familiar with "parking chairs." These are usually a folding chair (or another object, like a trash can or traffic cone) left in a parking spot to reserve it. Usually after a large snowfall, people spend a lot of time and energy digging out their cars and want to save that spot. Moving a parking chair and taking someone's spot is done at one's own risk, and cases of vigilante vandalism are common. Even though most cities have outlawed the behavior, it persists as an ad hoc solution to a problem that the transportation system is not designed to manage.

Scofflaw cycling is similar—it's a symptom of a system that is not working for its users. To fix this, the first step is getting people to understand the situation. That means getting out and riding a bike, experiencing the lack of infrastructure, the fear, and the confusion. The next step is fixing the system to accommodate all users.

Rethinking Our Streets

Changing streets is central to the pandemic bike boom story. Of the fifty-five largest cities in the United States, thirty responded to the pandemic with some type of street experiment aimed at shifting streets from a focus on moving traffic to becoming spaces for people.[32] Street experiments could be anything from improvements to basic infrastructure, such as sidewalks and bike lanes, to the creation of slower streets or closure of streets to cars. Streets can be closed either permanently or for short terms or special occasions, an action popularized by the tactical urbanism movement.[33] Details are vague, but pandemic street experiments were most often "open street" or "slow street" measures—short-term full or partial street closures. Open streets were typically single-day events during which a street was completely closed to cars. Slow streets were often multiday or multiweek measures, tended to restrict cars to local traffic only, and often included a network of streets.

In the early days of the pandemic, everything for which bike advocates have long fought seemed to materialize instantly, in sharp contrast to the slog of impact studies, permitting processes, city council meetings, and budgetary reviews facing bike projects in nonpandemic times. Just as traffic engineers were shocked as traffic disappeared overnight, bike advocates were shocked by the responsiveness of local leaders to remaking streets.

The pandemic was a street-level accelerator that communities, cities, and nonprofits leveraged to get things done. For example, Portland, Oregon; Austin, Texas; and Washington, DC, already had extensive plans to continue the improvement of their transportation systems; the pandemic just fast-tracked them. The circumstances of the pandemic made space, literally and figuratively, for urban experimentation, collaboration, and capacity building in cities.

By early 2022, Portland had added nearly 12.5 miles (20 kilometers) to its bikeway network and two new bike/pedestrian bridges over inner-city highways. The city also improved some existing bicycle infrastructure, including converting unprotected bike lanes to buffered bike lanes, improving intersections, and reducing speed limits and vehicle lanes on many streets. Portland also expanded its bikeshare system and converted it to all e-bikes. Austin made similar significant improvements to its bicycle infrastructure during the pandemic, adding almost 62 miles (100 kilometers) of bicycle facilities citywide, including lanes and paths, and building over thirty protected intersections that slow vehicles and improve safety for cyclists. And Washington, DC, continued expanding its bikeway network and lowered the city speed limit to 20 miles per hour.

In the 2000s, proponents of tactical urbanism established the idea of creating temporary changes in the built environment to garner support and advocate for permanent community change. Their playbook—simple and cheap street experiments—was applied nationally. Their simple presence has changed the conversation about cities, streets, and mobility.[34]

Today, 15-minute city and car-free street concepts are being piloted in places like Paris and Barcelona. Barcelona has begun implementing a Superblock model to reduce vehicle traffic in neighborhoods and provide more space for people.[35] In Paris, car-free zones have been established in front of schools and day care centers, and a portion of the Right Bank of the Seine, once a six-lane arterial, has been closed to private vehicles. And there are plans to pedestrianize the Champs-Elysées.[36] Today, ideas like this are discussed openly—as viable possibilities—in progressive American cities. Because of the pandemic, people have demanded more from their cities, and many cities have responded. In so doing, we find ourselves more capable than ever before of questioning the underlying assumptions of how our cities function and whose needs they should meet.

Rethinking Work

Around twenty-three million jobs were lost at the start of the pandemic as a result of closures and restrictions.[37] Those job losses were disproportionately among women, minorities, and those with lower levels of educational attainment and were concentrated in the service and hospitality sectors. So-called essential workers, facing increased risks of exposure to the coronavirus,[38] continued working in person—in fields as varied as health care and food service. In the meantime, and in addition to those who lost their jobs and were at home, millions of Americans who were used to heading to the office every day switched to remote work.

The most obvious consequence of remote work and job loss was that downtowns emptied of the people who no longer had any reason to go there. The downtowns of American cities—called central business districts by planners—were built for office workers, and without those workers they no longer had any purpose.

American downtowns were not doing well before the pandemic. Office spaces were struggling for tenants, and downtown retailers and businesses were struggling for customers. Suburban malls in the 1950s and then big-box stores in the 1980s were already drawing customers from downtowns. The advent of online retail further exacerbated these trends, and the pandemic just made them more obvious.[39] In a few weeks, the pandemic accelerated a decline that had been underway for decades. It is now impossible to ignore the fact that the daily ebb and flow of workers into and out of downtowns was never a sign of a healthy city but rather of a city on life support, a city that had for decades ignored and isolated communities of color living in downtowns in favor of the professional White commuter class. The required physical presence of so many people in the office—like emergency chest compressions—was the only thing keeping cities alive. Without them, downtown economies crashed harder and faster than anyone thought was possible.

In the meantime, cities trying to recover are grappling with what may become permanent changes to work life. Three years after the start of the pandemic, the Pew Research Center published a report finding that about one-third of those with jobs that could be done remotely were still working fully online and about four in ten were working hybrid schedules, partly online and partly in person.[40] People are returning to the office, but there is some regional variation; for example, as of 2023, Austin led the United States with about 65 percent of pre-pandemic office occupancy, while San Jose, California, came in last, with 31 percent of pre-pandemic office space occupied.[41] It may partially depend on industry. Like San Jose, San Francisco has faced a sluggish recovery from the pandemic, likely a combination of tech workers' ability to work remotely and high housing costs pushing many to move away at the start of the pandemic and not return.[42]

This means that downtowns dominated by empty office buildings are in a post-pandemic crisis. Demand for both office space and downtown retail spaces has dropped sharply and is unlikely to return to pre-pandemic levels. Cities are seeing the effects of vacant office space in reduced property taxes and, secondarily, in reduced sales taxes from downtown businesses that formerly catered to office workers.[43]

So what do we do about downtowns? Downtown real estate owners want everything back to normal and their buildings to make them money. All data points indicate that is not going to happen. Then the obvious solution is to change, to adapt. Pre-pandemic, the recipe for struggling downtowns was to include mixed-use development, with a focus on arts and cultural institutions, multimodal transportation options, and pedestrian-friendly development, ideally with some affordable housing.[44]

Adapting office buildings to more flexible uses such as housing will help address the housing crisis in the United States. Our cities desperately need affordable housing; it is estimated that the United States has a shortage of seven million affordable rental units and that eleven million households spend half of their income on rent.[45] Data from the website Zillow shows that rents were steadily increasing before the pandemic, at a rate of about 4 percent per year, nationally. By 2021, rents had nationally spiked by an additional 20–30 percent, depending on the region of the country.[46]

But the pandemic may have also accelerated the division of cities into haves and have-nots, making change more difficult for many cities. Bigger cities with more robust and diverse economies will find the funding, the markets, and the political support for revitalizing downtowns into more diversified and resilient places.[47] But smaller and midsize cities, those that struggled before the pandemic, will likely continue to struggle.[48]

A study by researchers from Wayne State and Michigan State Universities interviewed planners in small and midsize cities and found that downtowns were facing the same problems as before the pandemic—regulatory obstacles and a lack of either public or private money—suggesting that despite the fact that these planners know what needs to happen, they are unable to enact change. The study authors stated: "For many, the 'new normal' would, as much as possible, closely resemble the 'old normal' for their city centers."[49]

Adapting our downtowns means retrofitting office spaces for a variety of other uses, adapting laws and zoning to allow for alternative uses, investing in transit, and making streets more welcoming to people on foot or bike. It also means finding ways to bring life to downtowns outside of normal business hours. Cities have made this happen by simply increasing the diversity of uses and options in downtowns.

Melbourne, Victoria, Australia, may be the most famous example of this. In the 1990s, the city began converting downtown alleys ("laneways" in Australia) from underutilized spaces to a network of thriving public spaces—pedestrian thoroughfares lined with cafés and restaurants. The lesson from Melbourne is simple: we need to allow for more flexibility in the form and function of our downtowns for them to thrive in today's world of remote work and urban revitalization. The bicycle allows this to happen by freeing up spaces (parking lots, garages, and wide streets) previously devoted to cars.

US cities are taking their first tentative steps to do so. Chicago and Washington, DC, are experimenting with tax incentives and grant programs to facilitate downtown mixed-use and additional housing. New York City is considering, in addition to similar moves, rezoning parts of downtown Manhattan to allow residential construction.[50] Seattle, Pittsburgh, and Denver are also working with developers to convert existing downtown office spaces into housing.[51] Such programs may lack the sweeping vision of Melbourne's reimagining its alleys, but they are progress in the right direction. The hope is that if successful, these, or programs like them, can be transformative.

Centre Place laneway, Melbourne, Victoria, Australia. (Credit: City of Melbourne)

As much as Americans need affordable housing, we just as desperately need basic public transportation.[52] The American Public Transportation Association estimates that 45 percent of Americans have no access to public transportation, despite the fact that it is ten times safer per mile than driving, and every dollar invested in public transit generates five dollars for local economies.[53] But investing in transit or embarking on large-scale building retrofits is expensive and, as is often the case with public transit, a political nonstarter in states dominated by conservative legislatures.

Proof of Concept

Pandemic street experiments demonstrated that cities are as resilient and adaptable as the people who live there. Just as the bike boom demonstrated the potential for people to change the way they travel, pandemic-era street experiments demonstrated what cities can do to meet the needs of their residents. However, as the pandemic recedes into memory and COVID-19 into the background, we are also seeing how quickly the status quo can reassert itself.

During the pandemic, there was a powerful appetite for feel-good stories about our resilience and ability to triumph over adversity. Cities could host street fairs and enact low-cost street experiments that allowed for social distancing, physical activity, and relative safety from an airborne virus. Farmers

A pedestrianized street with paint, chairs, and tables in Brooklyn, New York. (Credit: Street Plans)

markets, food trucks, and cafés set up on closed roads were increasingly common, bringing people together and saving local businesses.

But an accurate accounting of what was done, and what remains today, is difficult to come by. The same study that found that thirty of the fifty-five largest US cities enacted some type of street experiments at the start of the pandemic found that six months later, only half of those cities had continued these efforts to improve streets.[54] As of this writing, in 2023, there is no comprehensive accounting of pandemic-related street improvements. But just as important as what happened in our cities during the pandemic was how it happened. Jobs for many moved online,[55] education moved online,[56] medical services moved online,[57] and community engagement did so as well.[58] Meetings of planning boards, city council meetings, and dozens of other city processes were suddenly broadcast on Zoom for anyone to participate. While most of the workings of government are technically open to the public, in practice they often take place at odd times and in hard-to-reach places, making access especially difficult for those without a car or job flexibility and who may also be caregivers. Moving the process online made outreach more inclusive than ever before.[59]

The lack of accounting and follow-through is troubling for all of us who celebrated a brief moment when it seemed that cities were listening when we, collectively, demanded places for people. At a minimum, the pandemic taught us that cities can hear and respond quickly to the needs of more members of our community. Slowing streets, improving parks, or painting bike lanes does not need to take years. As a result of the pandemic, the public now knows this. The potential is there, and the proof of concept is done. The challenge is in carrying momentum to continue beyond the pandemic.

Given that most of the world either lives in an urban area or is likely to do so soon, cities are where change needs to happen. Humans are creatures of habit. Our cities are built to accommodate and perpetuate our habits accordingly: there was no chicken or egg, just a coevolution of our behavior and our environment resulting in today's cities. The challenge today is to harness what we know about the problems we are facing, the solutions that have been pilot-tested during the pandemic, and our own propensity to revert to what feels comfortable. We can't ignore the lessons of the pandemic. We can recognize the potential for cities to change, rapidly and for the better. The worst thing we can do is slip back into the "old normal."

2

E-Bikes: Changing the Game

THE NETHERLANDS AND DENMARK HAVE HAD DECADES to experiment, to enable residents to experience the benefits of bicycle urbanism, and to enshrine good urbanism in the policy process. The United States has to get to work and play catch-up. E-bikes could be exactly what the country needs in order to do so.

E-bikes are more than just bikes. E-bikes reduce barriers to riding, making bikes viable car replacements for more people than regular bicycles ever could. E-bikes retain many of the transportation benefits of cars but use much less space and far fewer resources while being much safer for everyone. E-bikes can return us to human-scaled and human-centered places by bridging the gap between car-centric cities and car-free living. The data suggest this may already be happening.

In 2020, e-bikes began to take over the bike industry. In that year, global e-bike sales increased by over 40 percent.[1] That is one reason why Janette Sadik-Khan, former commissioner of the New York City Department of Transportation, who most notably converted Times Square into a pedestrian plaza, said, "The future transportation revolution is already here—and she arrived on an e-bike."[2]

Just a Bike

What is so special about an e-bike? To begin with a formal description and legal definition, it is simply a standard bicycle with a small electric motor. In most cases, the electric motor engages only when the rider is pedaling (rather than with a throttle as with a motorcycle or moped). E-bikes are not cheap, ranging in cost from as little as $500 to over $3,000. That's comparable to the cost of most quality entry-level standard bicycles. E-bikes are cheap compared with cars, however.

The bike industry lobbying group PeopleForBikes has, for legislative purposes, grouped e-bikes into three classes: (1) pedal-assisted e-bikes, with no throttle and a 20 miles per hour (mph) maximum speed; (2) e-bikes that are pedal assisted but also have a throttle to push the bike up to 20 mph without pedaling; and (3) e-bikes that are pedal assisted with no throttle and a maximum speed of 28 mph. PeopleForBikes recommends that the first two classes of e-bikes be allowed anywhere a regular bicycle can go, whereas a Class 3 e-bike should be permitted only on roads.

The potential for e-bikes begins with the bike itself. It is just a bike—or it is still a bike—but it is also unique, incomparable to the bikes that came before it. With the attachment of a small electric motor, it takes on a distinct set of characteristics that broaden its appeal and its utility. It is both familiar and new, exciting but not threatening. You don't need to be a cyclist to get an e-bike, just as you don't need to be a gearhead to get a car. Most drivers do not really care too much about cars; it's only a tiny subset of the population who gets really *into* cars. This is similar to the situation with bicycles in many European countries: biking is just another way to get around, like walking or taking transit, but with its own specific benefits over those modes. Some people are really into bikes, but it is not a prerequisite in cities that already have multiple viable options for transport.

E-bikes are breathing new life into bicycling by providing a new take on an old technology. They have the sparkle and promise of a new gadget but do not demand a religious devotion to a two-wheeled lifestyle. An e-bike is glossy and aspirational without being off-putting or out of reach. It is still a bicycle, so no special skills are necessary to ride.

E-assist motors can open up bicycles as transportation for more people than standard bicycles can. There is an expanding marketplace of e-bikes for those with disabilities that overlaps with an expanding range of micromobility options that are also purpose-built for those with certain disabilities (see chapter 4). Generally termed, adaptive e-bikes—those e-bikes designed with disabilities in mind—do not fit neatly into e-bike categories and instead exist somewhere between mobility scooters, wheelchairs, e-bikes, microcars, and even all-terrain vehicles.[3]

For people worried they are not fit enough to ride, the e-assist helps to dispel those concerns. For families, cargo bikes with e-assist can replace a car for most trips around town (see chapter 3). An e-bike can be a new (or additional) ride for cyclists, but, more important, an e-bike is simply a good way to get around.

For e-bikes to be a true game changer, people need to be able to use them as a viable car replacement and thereby better understand the potential for cities beyond automobile dependence. That is, more people need the opportunity to experience an e-bike and also to take note of how their communities can improve to make riding one safe and convenient. This understanding then needs to be translated into effective policy to reshape our cities.

Car Replacement

Ideally, more and more people can reach for the e-bike battery than for their car keys every morning. In turn, people can organize their lives to take advantage of their new e-bike's capabilities. People need flexible and inexpensive means of transportation for daily travel, which consists primarily of short trips. The Bureau of Transportation Statistics reported that in 2021, 52 percent of daily trips (by all modes) in the United States were under three miles.[4] Bicycle advocates often point to this as proof of the potential for bicycles to replace cars. The e-bike is just as flexible as a car when it comes to getting you where you want to go, when you want to go there.

Crucial to e-bikes replacing cars for short trips is the ability to use them safely in cities that are hostile to bikes. The lack of density in American cities means distances between destinations are greater, and often the most direct routes lack adequate cycling infrastructure. Therefore, using a standard bicycle for transportation in the United States has required people to ride farther to find safer paths to their destinations. By making bicycling easier, e-bikes may provide a work-around. In the absence of high-quality bike infrastructure, being freed from the physical challenges of a standard bike means more options for getting where you need to go.

Topography, temperature, ability, and fitness become less significant factors on an e-bike. Many American cities do have safe and pleasant bike infrastructure, in the form of multiuse paths and recreational trail networks. While they rarely connect destinations by the most direct route, they are calm and safe places to ride. With an e-bike, riders are able to piece together longer routes on safer infrastructure over more direct routes on dangerous and busy streets.

A large European study of e-bike use in seven cities found that e-bike users take longer trips than those taken on standard bicycles.[5] So the reality of using recreational paths and trails to get to where you need to go is possible. If people are willing and able to travel longer distances so they can use better infrastructure, then US cities can mitigate some of the barriers to bicycling created by auto-oriented cities.

A family outing with an e-bike and an e-cargo bike. (Credit: Erik Eagleman)

An Army on Two Wheels

In 2022, the *Wall Street Journal* ran an article with the headline "The Hottest New Car on the Market Is an E-Bike."[6] If the hottest new car is an e-bike, then who's buying? Unfortunately, it's hard to say. Industry data give us raw numbers but sparse demographics on buyers. The few studies available report results from surveys in which the majority of respondents are in their mid-fifties. It's unclear whether this is because older people are more likely to take surveys (i.e., have more free time), are more likely to own e-bikes (i.e., have more money and flexibility in how and when they travel), or both.[7] In two of those studies, researchers from Portland State University found that the number one reason people purchased e-bikes was to "replace car trips."[8]

Given that the Netherlands is a leader in cycling, it is helpful to look at Dutch trends to get a sense of the potential for e-bikes. Research from the Netherlands Institute for Transport Policy Analysis shows that e-bikes are increasingly being bought by younger people and used for transportation. A Dutch study that tracked individual e-bike usage over time (2013–2017) found that early adopters of e-bikes were older people riding for fun and exercise. But over the study period, the greatest growth in e-bike riding was among working women with children and among younger people and students. These growing rider groups were primarily riding e-bikes for transportation.[9] This trend seems to be catching on globally in more auto-dependent countries. A 2020 study of e-bike usage globally found that they are increasingly replacing car travel in North America and Australia. The researchers looked at trends in mode share—that is, the percentage of trips per day in a given place taken by different modes of transportation: car, bus, foot, or bike. The study found that in auto-dependent countries like the United States and Australia, people appear first to shift from a conventional bike to an e-bike and then gradually to use the e-bike as a substitute for driving.[10]

The key is scalability: How much driving can be replaced by e-bikes? The trend lines all point in the right direction. As Bloomberg's CityLab reported in 2023, the rise in e-bikes is "building an army of bike-lane advocates."[11]

The prospect of an army on two wheels is exciting for all of us in the business of making cities better. Traditional bike advocacy can harness the enthusiasm of new riders to improve our cities, translating the firsthand experiences and challenges of new riders navigating in cities not designed for bikes into real policy and infrastructure change. Just as the bike industry is rapidly evolving to meet the needs of new e-bike riders, however much they may differ from traditional cyclists, the bike advocacy world is also working to adapt.

With the variety of people and purposes that e-bikes could cater to continuing to expand, the potential is there, but it might be in places and in cases that do not directly align with existing local advocacy goals.

I spoke with Bill Nesper, executive director of the League of American Bicyclists, about the potential of this new army of e-bike-riding bike-lane advocates, and he was cautiously optimistic. We talked first about the transformative power of experiencing one's community on two wheels, whether e-assisted or not. Things like traffic that is too fast, bike lanes that abruptly end without warning, and lack of bike parking are obvious to anyone. He said that as he travels around the United States working with local advocates and educators, he sees more people on e-bikes and that there is "a sparkle in their eyes: this e-bike has changed things" for them.

Bill considers a part of the work of the league to bring together the old-guard cyclists with the new e-bike army—"to channel the strength of some of these new enthusiasts." In part, that means helping traditional bike advocates understand that e-bikes are not a threat. Beyond that, it means helping advocates work toward greater equity, justice, and inclusivity in their practices and outcomes. As he said, "bicycling culture needs to be about riding together."

Bill is especially hopeful about the potential of bike advocacy to leverage its strengths and connect with like-minded causes. He said that while the bike lobby may not have the money or the numbers, it absolutely has the enthusiasm and the dedication. This is what sets bicycle advocates apart from other like-minded groups. Members of the League of American Bicyclists—traditional cyclists—are "local changemakers" who care deeply, and that passion is their greatest strength.

The potential is clear for complementary causes and a broad coalition to come together, making use of existing advocacy pathways to enact real change. The dedication and enthusiasm that Bill is so proud of can be channeled into building broader coalitions to advocate for better cities and more inclusive urbanism. Partnering with groups advocating for better transit services or pedestrian infrastructure makes sense. But the collaborative potential and range of needs and interests of the new army of bike advocates can expand far beyond transportation. New coalitions, brought together by e-bikes, can address broad and systemic challenges plaguing cities, including zoning codes and regulations, housing policy, food access, and universal design (i.e., designing for accessibility for all people).

Changing the Industry

In 2021, sales of e-bikes in the United States grew by 240 percent while sales in the rest of the US cycling industry grew by only 15 percent.[12]

E-bike technology improved dramatically during the past decade. The batteries became cheaper, lighter, and longer lasting. These improvements translated into the first wave of e-assist road and mountain bikes, which were fitness-oriented offerings from major bike brands. The addition of pedal assistance was initially marketed to older recreational riders. The e-bike gave shops a product that kept their customers from aging out of the sport, and it was sold accordingly.[13] E-assist meant not only that lifelong cyclists could still ride as they aged but also that they could continue to ride after significant health events like surviving cancer. E-bikes also allow fitter cyclists and their less-fit partners to ride together. From a health perspective, e-bikes allow people to remain connected to friends and stay active much later in life than previously possible.

Increasingly, e-bikes are marketed to those who already ride but want a performance boost; they are a way for cyclists to have more fun putting in more miles with less effort. Regardless of the reason, more affluent aging baby boomers have driven the market for fitness-oriented e-bike purchases. These buyers prove that there are a lot of people who want to ride for exercise, and an e-bike can help them do so.

To grow the market for e-bikes, bike manufacturers and bike shops have been marketing their e-bikes to younger cohorts of existing riders. It's a start, but it's a shortsighted strategy. Attracting more existing riders to switch to e-bikes (or add an e-bike to their collection) ignores e-bikes' mass appeal as well as the e-bikes' attributes as car replacements.

The fact that the bike industry has focused on recreational riding is not surprising. It is symptomatic of wider problems in the industry, which has historically been an insular, exclusive, and closed ecosystem. For example, the industry has traditionally broken the bike world down into two camps: recreational riders and utilitarian (or transportation) riders—that is, those riding for sport and those riding to get to work. To say that *the* historical divide in cycling is between recreational riders and utilitarian (or transportation) riders is myopic at best. It's like saying *the* historical divide in food is between New York–style and Chicago-style pizza, as if pizza were the only food. Looking at cycling this way means accounting for only a small segment of Americans—educated, active, White, affluent, and mostly male—historically considered the only market (or the only market that mattered) for bicycles in the United States. The hope, and the potential, is that e-bikes can change this.

Torrance Strong thinks so. A Louisiana native and board member of the League of American Bicyclists, Torrance got his start in cycling as a bail bondsman in New Orleans. He realized he could process bonds faster than other bondsmen by bike. This resulted in his own business and a lifelong passion for bike advocacy, especially in places that may be forgotten in conversations about promoting bicycling, such as his hometown of Monroe, Louisiana. Monroe is a city of approximately fifty thousand in northern Louisiana near the borders of Arkansas and Mississippi, a region commonly referred to as the Ark-La-Miss. His bicycle advocacy work takes him across the United States as he tries to bring the message that bicycling can work for anyone, anywhere.

I first met Torrance in 2017 in Lincoln, Nebraska, on one of his advocacy tours and caught up with him again five years later. He is enthusiastic about e-bikes but also sees some tension between the old-guard cyclists he is used to working with and the new e-bike riders he's meeting on the road. He said, "There's a clash there. The thing about it, which is great, is that the 'share the road' mantra is getting tested." That is, can bikes share the road with e-bikes?

He told me about the overlooked potential for e-bikes in places like the rural South, how places like Monroe are perfect for recreational riding. The area is pancake-flat, with small towns every five to ten miles, connected mainly by smooth, two-lane roads with wide shoulders. He outlined a few reasons why bicycling has never caught on. The first is that "cycling in the South is still about stigma. If you're on a bicycle, you're poor." Despite the stigma, Torrance sees a lot of interest in cycling, and in e-bikes in particular, because the second barrier to more riding is baseline fitness. It's a big ask to try to convince someone who has never ridden a bike to do a ten-mile ride to the next town and back.

The math changes with an e-bike. The research is clear that riding an e-bike counts as exercise,[14] and Torrance is hopeful that excitement and interest about e-bikes will get more people in more places out and riding. He is also hopeful that more people riding new e-bikes will translate to less stigma about bicycles. And Torrance is particularly happy to see how the bike industry is changing to recognize unmet demand for e-bikes.

Bike brands and bike shops have been slow to recognize that the market for e-bikes goes well beyond their standard customer base. Millions of Americans could use e-bikes for exercise as well as transportation, but the standard bike shop model hasn't served them. In that vacuum, direct-to-consumer (DTC) companies have sprung up, offering a wide range of low-cost e-bikes (in some cases as low as $500 for a new e-bike) marketed to new groups of potential users and delivered almost fully assembled. In short, the options and pathways to e-bike ownership are expanding beyond the traditional brick-and-mortar bike shop model.

Being on a bike can begin a process of behavioral change that can evolve as people experience the potential of e-bikes. Going on weekend coffee shop rides can evolve into riding to work when the weather is nice. Leaving the car at home means saving on gas and could eventually mean deciding to go from a two- to a one-car household. Public health professionals refer to this as stages of change in the transtheoretical model of behavioral change.[15] It can apply to quitting smoking or starting to ride an e-bike. It begins with contemplation (e.g., noticing that riding an e-bike looks like fun) and proceeds to action (e.g., buying and riding an e-bike) and then maintenance and habituation of the new activity. The behavioral change process is scalable. If enough people under similar conditions are presented with a viable option for behavior that meets their needs and has few barriers to entry, it can be leveraged for larger societal changes.

Translating Enthusiasm into Action
Evolving away from auto dependence and transitioning to car-free cities means enacting effective policies. The first step is building interest in

e-bikes, which means making it easier for people to try, or buy, an e-bike. Bikeshare systems seem to be playing an important role in this process—giving people a chance to try an e-bike. Since about 2018, bikeshare systems across the country have been integrating e-bikes into their fleets or switching entirely to e-bikes.[16] The North American Bikeshare & Scootershare Association reported that from 2019 to 2021, the number of bikeshare systems deploying e-bikes jumped from about 25 percent to 50 percent nationally, and e-bikes were ridden 36 percent more than regular bikes.[17] It may seem like a slow way to build a movement, but it appears to be helping. Alongside increasing e-bike sales, e-bike enthusiasm is taking over bike advocacy priorities.

The buzz around e-bikes is translating into new bike policies in cities and states and even some hope for federal policy that supports cycling. As bikeshare systems convert to electric fleets, cities are pushing e-bike incentive programs to boost ownership. People are excited about e-bikes. Voting constituents want e-bikes, and their elected representatives are listening. The narrative is clear and doesn't require a background in urban planning to understand. As Noa Banayan, director of federal affairs at PeopleForBikes, told me, "We give you money, you go and ride an e-bike. It's straightforward. Whereas building bike infrastructure [to promote bicycling] is a tougher sell . . . e-bikes are new and sexy. Fighting for bike lanes is the opposite of sexy."

Cameron Bennett, a graduate student at Portland State University, created an e-bike incentive program tracker in 2021. As of this writing in 2023, the tracker has logged over 100 incentive programs across the United States and another 20 in Canada.[18] Incentive programs come in all shapes and sizes. There are rent-to-own programs, tax incentives, vouchers, and rebate schemes operating or in development at local and state levels. Some are dependent on income, while others are open to anyone purchasing an e-bike.

Denver's e-bike incentive program is considered one of the most generous and most successful, offering a $400 rebate on an e-bike and an additional $500 toward an e-cargo bike, while low-income Denverites can qualify for a $1,200 rebate on an e-bike, or $1,700 for an e-cargo bike.[19] Perhaps most important, the rebates are taken at the point of sale. The incentive program appears effective at getting e-bikes to new riders: a study conducted by the

City of Denver found that 30 percent of those claiming rebate vouchers had not previously ridden a bike.[20]

Unfortunately, successful e-bike incentive programs at the state level have not translated to success at the federal level in the United States. It is not new for bike advocates to struggle to be heard on Capitol Hill. The car has been central to national transportation policy since its inception,[21] and that has always meant huge projects, huge budgets, and a lot of press. If bike policy resulted in more ribbon cuttings and factory visits, things might be different. It is a vicious political cycle in which the absence of bicycle policies means nothing to campaign on. In turn, there's no history of campaigning on successful bicycle policies to push politicians to introduce bicycle legislation.

Meanwhile, as bike advocates struggle for traction at the national level, the auto industry has hijacked the conversation about the future of sustainable transportation to sell electric vehicles (EVs). According to Banayan, the auto industry has been very successful in distracting policymakers with the promise of EVs as a silver bullet.

EV lobbying has already had real policy consequences for e-bikes—the Inflation Reduction Act of 2022 discarded earlier draft legislation that would have included federal incentives for e-bikes and instead offers incentives only for electric vehicles. The hope is that future legislation can revive e-bike incentives, but in the meantime, this illustrates the overpowering influence of EVs as a barrier to sustainable urbanism.

After all, EVs are still cars. Just like gasoline-powered cars, they cost a lot of money. They still kill people, and pairing high-torque electric engines with massive battery packs makes them much more dangerous than conventional cars.[22] They don't burn gas, but they do require the construction and maintenance of roads, highways, and parking lots. All that infrastructure is spread out, which in turn stretches all the other infrastructure in our cities longer distances for fewer people than in more compact places. Building and maintaining all that infrastructure is resource intensive and emits significant quantities of carbon dioxide and other greenhouse gases. One important way to reduce the carbon footprint of our cities is to increase the efficiency of our existing infrastructure to meet the needs of more people with fewer cables, pipes, and pavement. An increased density of people served per mile of existing infrastructure is another reason why cities are so much more sustainable than suburbs.

As noted earlier, although EVs don't produce tailpipe emissions, they do require massive batteries. Production of EV batteries consumes vast quantities of minerals such as copper, cobalt, and lithium. The environmental consequences and human rights abuses that occur during the mining of these minerals are well documented,[23] but the EV industry has supercharged these problems while greenwashing its products.[24]

Yes, e-bikes also rely on batteries that use the same minerals and rely on the same supply chains, but we have to start somewhere. An EV battery weighs around 1,000 pounds, while an e-bike battery weighs about 10 pounds. You can make a lot more e-bike batteries instead of a single EV battery, and we can't let the perfect be the enemy of the good. In 2021, e-bikes outsold electric cars in the United States. An EV trade group estimated that 880,000 e-bikes were sold that year, compared with 608,000 electric cars.[25] While Capitol Hill remains distracted by EVs as a silver bullet, e-bikes are winning the hearts-and-minds campaign.

3

Cargo Bikes: Big, Slow, and Revolutionary

K*ari* A*nne* S*olfjeld* E*id is many things*, but she is emphatically not a cyclist. She is a designer, activist-turned-entrepreneur, and mother of five who, as she describes it, is "working to make cities loveable."[1] Doing so means making cities people centric. Centering cities on people means moving cars to the periphery and ensuring that residents have transportation options to reach the people and places they need to on a daily basis. For Kari Anne, doing so involves reducing automobile reliance by making cargo bikes more accessible. The company she cofounded, Whee!, has been making waves in the micromobility world by offering long-term leases on e-cargo bikes (cargo bikes with e-assist). The goal is to make these otherwise expensive bikes more accessible to young families in Oslo, Norway.

Kari Anne and I met at a tiny café called Kiosk! in Oslo's Galgeberg neighborhood, named after the gallows where justice was administered during the Middle Ages. Despite its name, the neighborhood is one of the most vibrant in Oslo. It is also one of the most diverse. Formerly a gas station built in 1935, Kiosk! sits at the corner of two streets intersecting at about a forty-five-degree angle. Where there was once a driveway at the tip of the angle for cars coming in for service, there is now outdoor seating covered by an aquamarine-painted overhang and surrounded by planters.

Even though it was nearly May, it was still too cold to sit outside, so we sat at the only two seats available in the café's interior. In 2021, the building was renovated through a crowdfunding campaign, and it is now an independent business with some sixty-five shareholders. A collaborative, community-based ethic is taking root in this corner of Oslo, which Kari Anne brings to her work—enhancing lives by enhancing access to urban mobility.

Kari Anne's ambitions are based in personal experience. She experienced the challenges, specifically transportation challenges, that come with raising kids in cities. Navigating streets, sidewalks, and buses with babies or young children is exhausting, both physically and mentally. Without a car, parents with children are more reliant on public transit and are at the mercy of routes and timetables. Her experience is illustrative of larger problems with transportation. Public transit is generally designed around the journey to work. Bicycles are primarily an option for single, able-bodied individuals. Given those limitations, it makes sense that families (and caregivers in general) rely heavily on cars.[2]

Faced with limited options for family mobility in the city, Kari Anne thought about moving to the suburbs; her family could get a bigger place for less money and use the savings to buy a car. But she recognized that relying on a car was antithetical to the way she wanted to live. She values a car-free urban lifestyle and strives to live sustainably, but that lifestyle is so often incompatible with family life.

The complexities of physically navigating city living with children and the cost of housing are often what drive young families out of cities. It's a decision I am familiar with, having grown up in the suburbs of Phoenix, Arizona, and, prior to moving to Oslo, having young kids in suburban Lincoln, Nebraska. Living in the suburbs as a young family in the United States felt less like a choice than the only option. The data suggest that my experience is shared by many others. Across the United States, young families tend to leave urban areas, and that trend accelerated during the COVID-19 pandemic.[3] The trend also cuts to a central problem for cities: cities are not designed for most people.

At their best, cities are vibrant and exciting places, but the prevailing conception of cities is also elitist and exclusionary—brimming with cultural events, bars, and cafés, a playground for the young, monied, and able-bodied. Part of making cities lovable means making them for everyone. It is a concept that is gaining traction in the United States (e.g., AARP's Livable Communities program[4]) and globally (e.g., 8–80 Cities[5] and the World Health Organization's Age-Friendly Cities initiative[6]). To do that means ensuring everyone is able to easily navigate to and through their communities to meet their daily needs. Cities take time to change, and building accessibility and convenience is an incremental process, but we need to get started.

For Kari Anne, the catalyst for making cities more friendly to families is the e-cargo bike. E-cargo bicycles are the closest thing families have to a complete car replacement, and they are perfect for cities. E-cargo bikes are more convenient and much less expensive to own and operate than a car. They require a fraction of the parking space and road space, and a sliver of the electricity. (See chapter 2.)

After buying her first e-cargo bike, Kari Anne did not become a cyclist, but she did become a cargo bike evangelist and an innovator in urban mobility. A cargo bike can carry kids, all their stuff, and groceries while easily tackling even hilly cities with an electric-assist motor. Kari Anne's cargo bike made it possible for her family to stay in the city they love while also introducing them to a more independent, active, and, most important, fun new lifestyle.

Fun is a crucial component to the success of cargo bikes. Kari Anne and I swapped stories of taking rides around the city with our kids in tow, enjoying the fresh air and the experience. I bought my first e-cargo bike a month before our meeting (and only three months after moving to Oslo with my wife and two young daughters). I was, and still am, enamored with the experience of exploring the city by bike as a family. Unlike Kari Anne, I was born into American automobile dependence, and I had spent the better part of my adult life trying to escape it.

My wife and I had always lived in places that required a car, so our first few months in Oslo were the first time we had tried car-free living with young kids. Getting everyone into the car had always been a struggle, but with our cargo bike, the kids would enthusiastically jump aboard. Riding the cargo bike with my kids is simultaneously invigorating and calming. It also happens to be the best way to get around a city with kids.

Kari Anne Solfjeld Eid demonstrating the capabilities of a mid-tail e-cargo bike. (Credit: Kari Anne Solfjeld Eid)

Cargo bikes have been gaining popularity for years, and the addition of electric assistance further amplified their rise. The e-cargo bike, alongside the e-bike, can be the antidote to the anti-urbanism of the past century. The cargo bike and e-cargo bike can meet the transportation needs of more people in more circumstances than cars or public transport. Accommodating cargo bikes creates broader opportunities for families to get around cities.

E-cargo bikes scale up the benefits of e-bikes (see chapter 2) and are viable car replacements for families. In Oslo, New York City, or Washington, DC, that might mean never buying a car in the first place. In Lincoln, Nebraska, or Phoenix, Arizona, cargo bikes can shift daily lives from car dependent to car-lite: maybe the car sits in the garage most of the week and comes out only on rainy days, or maybe a two-car household can sell a car and become a one-car household. Every little bit helps in trying to reduce auto reliance.

Kari Anne is quick to point out that despite what some might think, Norwegians also have had a long love affair with the car. Norway is a rugged country made up primarily of smaller cities and towns separated by forests, mountains, and water. Many Norwegians grow up in places where they need a car every day. While Oslo is a world leader in reducing auto dependence, it is the exception in Norway, not the rule. Kari Anne looks at auto dependence as a life event—a Faustian bargain in which people must choose between the lifestyle they so value and the material benefits of cheap square footage and a big car.

A Faustian bargain is characterized by tragedy, wherein whatever is gained is worth less than what it was traded for. Leaving the city also means leaving a social network and buying into a less sustainable, less active lifestyle. People are increasingly approaching it for what it is: an ethical dilemma, a lifestyle change forced on families by a society that does not provide adequate transportation or affordable housing for all. It's a deal with the devil in which the only option is to buy into a self-perpetuating and unsustainable system.

Kari Anne started Whee! in 2020 after realizing the transformative power of cargo bikes to help families in cities. She also wanted to reduce the barriers to entry for e-cargo bikes, specifically the up-front cost. So she created Whee! as a cargo bike leasing company. Whee! chose smaller, lighter, more city-friendly cargo bikes for its fleet. Unlike the Dutch cargo bikes with a large basket in front of the rider, Whee!'s bikes look more like a standard bike with a slightly longer tail end (the specific models they use are known as mid-tails, while longer versions of the same setup are known as longtail cargo bikes). The tail end of the bike can be set up with seats or benches for passengers or used for cargo. In total, these bikes can carry about 375 pounds. You can park a Whee! bike in a normal bike parking spot or maneuver it up or down a few stairs if needed. The bikes work well for compact apartments and urban living and are much easier to use than larger cargo bikes for smaller people, women, and those with no experience riding.

Beginning with a few dozen customers, Whee! piloted cargo bikes through a subscription service that includes everything—the bicycle and equipment (e.g., baskets, child seats, and racks), service, maintenance, and insurance—for a monthly rate. Whee!'s business model has been wildly successful. Bike leases are typically for two years, and Kari Anne is considering a lease-to-own option. Despite pandemic-related supply chain delays that limited its fleet size, Whee! has not stopped growing; it currently operates a fleet of almost three hundred bicycles. Since its inception, Whee! has struggled to keep up with demand.

What Is a Cargo Bike?

Cargo bikes are the gentle giants of the bike world. Like manatees serenely drifting through seagrass, they seem to calmly roll down the bike lane, quietly managing their massive bulk. They are simultaneously formidable and absurd in the way they can balance a whole family on two (or sometimes three) small bike tires. Cargo bikes were once rare outside a handful of European cities, but times are changing. With the widespread availability of electric-assist engines, cargo bikes are riding a wave of popularity at the nexus of the e-bike boom and the explosion of micromobility,[7] pandemic fears about transit,[8] and a revolution in freight and delivery services.[9]

The cargo bike is almost as old as the bicycle itself. It was likely first invented in England in 1877, entering more widespread use in Denmark and the Netherlands during the first part of the twentieth century after a number of innovations.[10] The bikes were generally specialized items built on demand by skilled builders. But cargo bikes have largely been a niche item, a footnote to the bicycle story, until recently.

Modern cargo bikes come in all shapes and sizes and are constantly being adapted to fit new needs. Most cargo bikes can carry about 100–200 pounds in addition to the rider. There are two general categories of cargo bikes: longtails and front loaders. As the names imply, longtails (and the shorter midtails, like the Whee! bikes) are regular bikes with a longer tail end, in which cargo is carried behind the rider. In contrast, front loaders have a large basket in front of the rider for cargo. Both types have their pros and cons, but the front-loading style is what most people associate with a cargo bike. The design comes from the earliest versions of these bikes, known as *bakfiets* (Dutch for "box-bikes"). The first models were popular in Denmark and the Netherlands and were essentially backward tricycles: they had a box between two wheels in the front, and the rider sat behind the box and over the third wheel. Two-wheeled box-bikes were later popularized, and the design became the basis for the modern front loader.[11]

Longtail cargo bikes are a more modern invention. They have a smaller footprint than the front-loading variety and handle more like a standard bicycle. Mid-tail versions, with a shorter tail end, are especially popular with city dwellers and those who lack the storage space necessary for the larger front-loading bikes. Some mid-tail bikes can fit in a standard bike rack or are specially designed to balance on their back wheel and be stored upright indoors.

Beyond the front-versus-tail dichotomy, cargo bikes are endlessly flexible in their designs, intended uses, and actual applications. It depends on the specific bike, but most cargo bikes can carry an additional adult or a few children and all their stuff. Most cargo bikes for personal use are designed to carry up to about four hundred pounds, including the person operating the bike. Both versions of the bikes can be outfitted in a variety of ways to meet a range of needs and preferences or reinforced for heavy loads. For example, the front box of a cargo bike can be left empty for more storage or fitted with seats and seat belts for kids. There are specialized child safety seats and baby carriers with additional built-in suspension. Cargo bike makers also sell enclosures and weather screens to protect kids and gear from rain and snow.

The popularity of cargo bikes is at an all-time high and continues to grow. Sales statistics are difficult to find for cargo bikes in the United States, but big American brands such as Trek, Cannondale, and Specialized are releasing their own e-cargo models in the United States, as are direct-to-consumer brands such as Aventon, Rad Power Bikes, and Lectric.[12] Globally, industry groups are throwing around crazy numbers in value and growth of e-cargo bikes. The global e-cargo bike market is estimated at about $2 billion today and is forecast to reach an estimated $11 billion in the next ten years.[13] These numbers may sound unbelievable, but they are based on what is currently happening in European markets, where e-cargo bike sales are booming for both personal use and freight and delivery. The European Cargo Bike Industry Survey estimated that almost 100,000 cargo bikes were sold in 2022 (compared with an estimated 17,000 sold in 2018).[14] The industry anticipates increasing growth in cargo bikes as their potential uses continue to expand.

European cargo bike producers have been making high-end car-replacement e-cargo bikes for at least the past decade. Their popularity in Europe spiked after the introduction of e-assist in the 2010s; a clear through line can be seen from the rising availability and popularity of e-assist to the e-cargo bike explosion in Europe. European consumers, already accustomed to the idea of transportation by bike, quickly realized the benefits of e-assistance and began buying e-bikes. In turn, as e-assist became standard on cargo bikes, families, older people, and those needing to transport more than a standard bike could carry caught on to the benefits of e-cargo bikes.

That through line—from transport cycling to e-assist to e-cargo bikes—is a demonstration of how new technologies or innovations catch on and spread, eventually becoming ubiquitous. The process of learning about something new, seeing it in your community, and eventually incorporating it into your own life can take time. It is also different in every neighborhood, city, and country.

Overcoming Barriers to Adoption

First proposed in 1962 by a social scientist named Everett Rogers, innovation theory describes how innovations spread: first by early adopters, then by early majority adopters and late majority adopters, and finally reaching the "laggards," who are the last to change their ways.[15] Innovation theory states that the key to uptake is that people need to be able to see evidence that the innovation can work for them before they accept it. Cell phones are a good example of innovation theory—once the technology was ready, they took time to catch on, but today they are ubiquitous.

The same process occurred with cargo bikes in cities across northern Europe during the past decade. A cargo bike with e-assistance is expensive, starting at about US$3,000. An e-cargo bike set up for kid carrying with child seats and so forth can reach US$5,000–$10,000. It is a significant investment, but not when compared with a car. According to Kelley Blue Book, the average price of a new car in the United States was about $50,000 in 2023. Even though the price of used cars leveled off after spiking during the pandemic, the average price of a used car was nearly $30,000. Still, asking people to spend thousands of dollars on a bicycle and use it as a car replacement and kid carrier is a tall order. People first need to see with their own eyes how cargo bikes can function in daily life in their own community. That is, what does it look like to take the kids to school by cargo bike? How much equipment can these bikes carry? Where do you store them at night?

American cities, and American culture, are not primed for bikes to catch on. Americans (and, more important, American policymakers) need to think of bicycles as transportation. In the aftermath of the pandemic bike boom and the rising e-bike boom the perception of bicycles is shifting, but it is taking time. Once people experience a lifestyle divorced from driving and made possible by an e-bike, the possibilities of an e-cargo bike come into focus.

Everything is big about cargo bikes. The bikes are big, the price is often big, and therefore the commitment is big. (It should be noted that high-quality nonelectric cargo bikes can be purchased from a number of manufacturers for around $1,000.) Convincing people, especially families who may be living in auto-dependent places, to spend thousands of dollars on a bicycle to transport their kids is a big ask. There are more questions and concerns for those interested families and fewer early adopters to look to, talk to, and learn from. As a result, cargo bikes are taking longer to catch on here than elsewhere.

Early adopter families in the United States tend to become ambassadors for the cargo bike lifestyle. I interviewed one early adopter and bike designer about the cargo bike lifestyle in the United States. Erik Eagleman is now based in Madison, Wisconsin, but lived in Europe throughout the mid-2000s, working in the bike industry. "When you commit to that kind of cost, you are committing to a lifestyle," Erik told me. In Europe, that meant deciding whether the cost justified the convenience of a cargo bike over public transit.

Erik bought an e-cargo bike from the Amsterdam-based company Urban Arrow, about a decade ago. The Urban Arrow is set up like a traditional Dutch cargo bike with a large basket in front, but that is where the similarities end. It has a streamlined profile, an enclosed drivetrain, and a cohesive look. The bike is big, one of the biggest family-focused e-cargo bikes, but also sporty. The carrying box in front is reminiscent of a speedboat's hull or an airplane's fuselage.

Erik described how Urban Arrow "took something somewhat archaic and made it amazing and sleek and introduced a whole genre of kid carrying, safety, and usability." Despite the cost, the Eagleman family decided to buy one while living in Europe—buying into an e-cargo bike lifestyle—and he was enamored with it. He told me, "Our lifestyle has followed the cargo bike ever since." The bike is convenient and attractive. It also allows for some much-needed low-stress family time. Having his kids in the box up front allows him to always have an eye on them and talk to them. The ride is a shared experience. Riding with his kids is like a distillation of all the positive aspects of driving with kids while all the negatives, the traffic, the noise, the stress, evaporate away.

When the Eagleman family moved back to the United States in 2014, they brought their bike with them. At the time, the Urban Arrow was not yet available in the United States, and Erik is proud to say he (likely) had the first one in the United States. The Eagleman family approached life in the United States from a different perspective after living in Europe, using a cargo bike as their primary means of transportation. Maintaining their lifestyle became a priority when they were house hunting in Madison. Their search became

The Eagleman family's Urban Arrow. (Credit: Erik Eagleman)

more about neighborhood access and safe bicycle infrastructure than square footage or yard size. Erik said he needed to find "a marriage of product [i.e., cargo bike] and environment" to support their lifestyle.

Erik had a lot to say about the benefits of the cargo bike lifestyle and sounded a lot like Kari Anne Solfjeld Eid. It is surprising because Madison, Wisconsin, is definitely a bike-friendly city, but nothing like Kari Anne's neighborhood in Oslo. Neither city is known for particularly good weather for riding. Nevertheless, in both cases, an e-cargo bike is a fun, active, and sustainable car replacement for most of these two families' daily needs. For Kari Anne, the cargo bike is a tool for remaining in the city and sustaining an urban life as her personal life changes. For Erik, the cargo bike is a means to bring an urban, car-lite lifestyle to the Midwest.

The cargo bike lifestyle is flexible and can mold to a variety of cities. The cargo bike itself is also flexible and can increase access to cycling for those traditionally ignored by the bicycle industry. For example, a small but growing niche of the cargo bike industry caters specifically to those with mobility challenges and families of children with disabilities. E-cargo bikes allow caregivers of older people a way to enjoy cycling. They also allow parents to ride with children who require specialized medical equipment and provides a way for people who are too often stuck inside a house or car to be out in their community and able to socialize with friends and neighbors.

I spoke to another early adopter, Lelac Almagor, a former teacher and mother of three living in Washington, DC. She had bought an e-cargo bike for her family a few years earlier and went from never riding a bike to putting twelve thousand miles on her cargo bike. She was so enamored with her new bike that she began working for the company that made it, Bunch Bikes, which has begun specializing in adapting cargo bikes to work with a range of special needs.

Just like Kari Anne, who started Whee! in Oslo, Lelac is emphatically not a cyclist. She is happy to be an early adopter of e-cargo bikes, although she struggled to find one that fit her needs. She wanted something comfortable and stable and easy to manage when loaded with kids. She eventually decided on a three-wheeler with two wheels in front and a large box between them. The front box and wheels pivot and are turned together to steer the bike by the rider, who sits behind the box. They are a bit slower than two-wheeled cargo bikes, and the rider has to make turns slowly, but they are very stable, and no balancing is required.

The three-wheeled design has been popular in northern Europe for decades and has proven ideal for a range of unique needs. Lelac told me that Bunch Bikes did not initially intend to market a bike for those with disabilities, but families began buying the bikes, adapting them themselves, and telling their friends. The bikes are sold online, direct-to-consumer (DTC); Lelac told me how the company eschewed traditional marketing or online advertising, instead creating a network of families who have bought the bike and are willing to talk to potential customers in their area, expanding the network of early adopters. "We see that pattern," she said. "One person in a town gets a bike, then suddenly that small town has eight bikes."

Lelac sees the diffusion of the cargo bike lifestyle in real time. She firmly agrees that the key to unlocking the potential of cargo bikes for families is seeing them in person and talking to like-minded people in similar circumstances. It removes the intimidation factor of the traditional bike shop. Everyday interactions, chance encounters, and personal connections dispel fears and offer judgment-free answers to questions. Many of the families with Bunch Bikes participate in an online owner's club where they share tips and "hacks" for a variety of situations and needs. For families whose cycling needs are largely ignored or misunderstood, this is the best way to determine whether a cargo bike will work for them.

The word "transformative" came up repeatedly in my conversation with Lelac and the stories she shared of families who had purchased e-cargo bikes. She described a wide range of uses for cargo bikes as adaptive vehicles that able-bodied people might not readily picture—for example, a parent with multiple sclerosis who cannot ride a two-wheeled cargo bike riding one with three wheels; riding with a child with severe autism for whom movement helps to avert meltdowns; riding with a child who needs to travel with oxygen, a gastrostomy tube, or a service dog; bringing a child's wheelchair on a bike so they can use it at their destination. Bunch Bikes hosts a blog on its website with many such stories to spread the word about the potential of cargo bikes to increase inclusion in the bicycle world.[16]

These examples speak to the potential of the cargo bike but also the pervasiveness of ableism in cities. Ableism presumes "able-bodiedness,"[17] but that is often shorthand for what Rosemarie Garland-Thomson, author of *Extraordinary Bodies*, describes as the presumed normal (or "normate") that is White, young, able, and heterosexual.

Lisa Stafford, an activist and a researcher at the University of Tasmania, Australia, has studied disability and urban planning extensively. She explains how cities obviously fail to meet the basic needs of people with disabilities in their form and function and how ableism permeates the process of planning our cities (i.e., planning decisions are made without input or representation from those with disabilities). Most important, failures of inclusion result in marginalization and constitute "exclusion by design."[18]

Within transportation—the ability to access the places and services you need when you need them—significant challenges face those with disabilities. Autonomous vehicle makers and ride-hailing services have for years claimed that their products and services would be "a boon for disabled customers."[19] Such claims are packed with assumptions about the capabilities of autonomous systems and the basic accessibility of autonomous vehicles (and the interfaces necessary to use them) by those with a range of needs. The potential may be there, but autonomous vehicle makers have yet to deliver.

Disability advocates worry, and rightly so, that in a push for livable cities and car-free cities, inclusion will be forgotten. The e-cargo bike is not a solution for everyone with a disability. Cargo bikes are not the only answer to addressing ableism in cities, just an adaptation to mitigate some of the consequences. Complex and omnipresent systemic challenges require multiple approaches and solutions. But the fact that the cargo bike is helping some individuals and families in unexpected ways is a first step. It is one more option to begin to address a complex problem.

Delivery by Cargo Bike

I had never spent much time thinking about how a package made it to my porch, how the electrician got to my house, or how toilet paper got to the grocery store, but all that changed during the pandemic.

The pandemic put our reliance on this previously unseen sector in stark relief, illustrating for all of us our dependence on fast and efficient deliveries of products and services as well as the traffic safety and climate change impacts of that dependence.

The pandemic did not cause our increasing dependence on urban freight, but it did accelerate existing trends in e-commerce, online retail, and home delivery of a range of products and services.[20] During the pandemic, urban freight became a lifeline for people at home and the businesses they were no longer frequenting. For a time, delivery workers were recognized as essential workers[21] and delivery trucks were often the only traffic on streets. But since the pandemic, America's love affair with home delivery has only grown, and the negative effects of delivery trucks are being felt in the form of increased congestion and pollution and worsening road safety.

Current estimates suggest that urban freight accounts for 10–15 percent of all miles traveled in cities. It is also the most costly and polluting link in the logistics chain.[22] The World Economic Forum estimated that the number of delivery vehicles will rise by nearly 30 percent by 2030, and those vehicles will account for 30 percent of emissions in cities. Corinne Kisner, executive director of the National Association of City Transportation Officials, said, "Managing the increasingly unsustainable influx of delivery vehicles on city streets will be key to creating vibrant, healthy, and sustainable cities."[23]

Cities can do their part by decarbonizing in any and every way possible. Cargo bikes as car replacement for families is an important piece of that puzzle, reducing household carbon footprints. But focusing only on people ignores the vast potential for cargo bikes. E-cargo bikes provide a flexible, safe, and sustainable platform for urban delivery. They are small and maneuverable, easily able to navigate around traffic jams and deliver to locations vans never reach. They can be configured to deliver mail and packages, building materials, or food, even refrigerated or frozen food.

The benefits of cargo bikes extend to those who work in trades that require them to carry tools or equipment but want to avoid traffic jams, fuel costs, and parking fees. The combined size, weight, and speed of these bikes also means they are much safer in the event of a collision. While electric delivery vans emit very few emissions per mile, they lack the flexibility and safety benefits possible with e-cargo bikes. Recent research confirms that cargo bikes can be a viable solution for urban freight: it is estimated that cargo bikes could replace half of the freight trips currently completed by vehicles in European cities while producing a fraction of the emissions.[24]

Just as the e-cargo bike trend among families began in Europe, so did the use of cargo bikes for freight and delivery. Major shipping companies have been piloting various incarnations of e-cargo bike delivery vehicles in European cities for the better part of a decade. For example, the global shipping company DHL has been using four-wheeled e-cargo bikes in more than eighty European cities and claims to have replaced 60 percent of its inner-city routes with e-cargo bikes.[25]

The trend is catching on in some US cities. Amazon (and its subsidiary Whole Foods Market), UPS, and DHL e-cargo bikes have started operating in New York City. There, they can operate on the cities' expanding bike infrastructure, and smaller cargo bikes can park on the sidewalk when making deliveries.[26] And in the Pacific Northwest, cargo bike enthusiasts have been running "disaster relief trials" since 2012, testing the viability of e-cargo bikes to deliver needed supplies in the event of a major earthquake or another disaster.[27]

Delivery by e-cargo bike is a very different process from delivery by truck or van. Traditionally, the biggest street-legal delivery vehicle is loaded with as much as it can hold each morning at a distribution center outside the city, and then it is driven around the city as its cargo is emptied. This approach is slow and inefficient. A large van requires a lot of fuel. Even if it is a hybrid or electric vehicle, it is still massive and heavy, making it dangerous around other road users. These vehicles are difficult to navigate and park in cities made for cars. Big and heavy vehicles are incompatible with an urban mobility future centered on people, bikes, and micromobility.

An urban mobility future that accommodates safe and efficient freight requires a completely different approach. Instead of having one massive distribution center that feeds a succession of large trucks on the urban periphery, shippers are creating networks of mini distribution hubs across cities. These mini hubs feed fleets of cargo bikes that are constantly delivering and refilling—making dozens of short trips, made faster by centralized distribution and less time spent loading and unloading, waiting in traffic, and parking. Hubs can be made in all shapes and sizes and do not necessarily need to be permanent structures; some companies simply park a delivery truck and use it as a hub.[28] In this way, cargo bikes act as an ideal supplement to shipping companies' existing fleets, infrastructure, and services.

The bikes are being adapted for this new role as well. A new wave of cargo bikes is being designed and engineered for the rigors of daily work. E-cargo bikes have historically been built as extensions of standard bikes. But parts and materials for cargo bikes designed for a person, or even a family, to ride daily are not suitable for carrying hundreds of pounds of cargo for twelve or more hours per day. Endless variations of stronger, more stable, and larger cargo bikes are introduced every year. DHL has its four-wheeled versions, but there are multiple formats with more or fewer wheels and front or rear loading.

Cargo bikes began as a tool for businesses and were only later adapted for carrying people. The first cargo bikes were service and delivery vehicles popular in the Netherlands and Denmark—flat places well suited to the bulky and heavy vehicles invented in the late nineteenth century. These same places have seen a resurgence of cargo bikes (prior to e-assist motors) since the 1990s.

I spoke with Jos Sluijsmans, founder and codirector of the International Cargo Bike Festival, about the rise of cargo bikes and what they can mean for service, delivery, and a decarbonized urban mobility future. Jos carved out a niche as a bicycle messenger on a cargo bike in the Netherlands long before electric assistance was available. While other messengers were riding fast bikes and delivering small packages and letters, he was bringing organic produce to stores and restaurants by cargo bike. A true early adopter in the modern cargo bike world, he recognized the potential for cargo bike delivery.

He enthusiastically described for me the myriad variations of purpose-built working cargo bikes and the growing list of businesses using them. The smallest businesses (such as small bakeries or repair companies) might use a single cargo bike to deliver goods or services or be based out of a single bike (like Jos's organic produce delivery service). The largest companies are those such as DHL and other global shippers that operate fleets of hundreds of bikes in multiple cities.

Delivery by cargo bike is not just for cities. There are already proven examples of e-cargo bikes working in small towns and rural areas. I interviewed Sam Starr, a logistics consultant based in Vancouver, British Columbia, who specializes in sustainable freight systems, and asked him about cargo bikes beyond big cities. He mentioned Cargodale, which operates a fleet of e-cargo bikes in small towns in the English Midlands. Cargodale's website says the company delivers "shopping, hot food, cold food, and lots more. We can navigate tiny lanes, zip round congestion, take on all the hills." Then there is curbwise, doing e-cargo bike delivery of "just about anything" to the region in and around Stevens Point, Wisconsin.

Sam explained, "You'll notice the common thing to their success is working with local markets, farmers, co-ops, and retailers." The system is similar to that of bigger cities. Small delivery companies in smaller communities utilize "micro-consolidation points" that are centered on the neighborhood level. It is a different system from one big delivery van driving from town to town, and it is more sustainable. Local businesses and growers can also forgo large-scale freight in general, either delivering goods to micro-consolidation points or having cargo bikes come to them. The flexibility and cost savings inherent in using bikes "further emphasize why neighborhood-oriented micro-logistics hubs work for cargo bikes, even when from the outset, the lack of density may seem like a deterrent."

When it comes to cargo bikes and freight, the whole is likely greater than the sum of its parts. That is, the ability to get a package delivered quickly and sustainably is good, but a city functioning around cargo bike delivery services could be great. If cargo bikes replace delivery vehicles, it will mean a reallocation of urban space. Traffic lanes will lose some of their largest and most dangerous users, and that traffic will be transferred to the bike lane.

But moving freight, delivery, and service vehicles from the car lane to the bike lane fundamentally alters the purpose of the bike lane. Jos said, "If cargo bikes replace vans (on roads), they should replace the space on the road." As working cargo bikes replace service and delivery vehicles but still use the bike lane, they are moving traffic problems from the road to the bike lane.

From a system perspective, it is counterproductive for delivery trucks to vacate vehicle lanes only to provide more space for cars. For working cargo bikes to be part of a new mobility solution in cities, working cargo bikes need to occupy the same space as the trucks and vans they are replacing. Doing so can start a process of altering street space.

The process begins with cargo bike services and delivery vehicles functioning as mobile traffic calming, taking the lane and slowing things down. Reducing the speed differential between vehicle lanes, bike lanes, and sidewalks improves safety for everyone while also making (former) car lanes more accessible to cyclists. The end goal is that over time, nonessential vehicle traffic will be made inefficient and crowded out of the roadway. An ideal streetscape in a car-lite future could include space for public transit, mixed uses, bike lanes, and sidewalks. Cargo bikes can be both beneficiaries of this transition and catalysts for accelerating it.

Changing Communities

Cargo bikes are a tool, like any other tool, and can be applied as needed wherever appropriate, even in US cities. The most exciting thing about the cargo bike revolution, for both families and freight, is that cargo bikes can ignite and accelerate changes in auto-oriented places.

Cargo bike delivery is already happening in Seattle, Boston, and New York City,[29] proving its viability in American cities. But there is no reason why e-cargo freight cannot work outside urban centers. E-cargo bike delivery is possible with either permanent or temporary hubs in small towns, on college campuses, or only in certain neighborhoods. Cargo bike delivery does not need to replace existing options but can begin by augmenting current services. The point is to use cargo bikes to increase sustainability in large and small ways. (See chapter 2.)

Cargo bike uptake, from early adoption to urban transition, is underway across the United States, demonstrating the merits of cargo bikes for all communities. For example, Bosch, one of the largest makers of e-assist engines globally, partnered with community groups in underserved neighborhoods in Chicago during the pandemic to pilot an e-cargo bike leasing service.[30] The bikes were used to deliver essentials like food and diapers in the Chicago neighborhoods of Belmont Cragin, Logan Square, North Lawndale, Englewood/Chatham, Bronzeville, and South Shore, providing vital services and maintaining neighborhood connections during lockdowns. The pilot program ran for only a few months, but according to Bosch, many of the community groups opted to purchase or lease the bikes. It remains to be seen what the future holds for this program and those like it, but the proof of concept is there.

Early adopter families are proof of how individual changes swell to become waves of community change. As of this writing in 2023, Lelac Almagor continues to rack up thousands of miles each year on her cargo bike with her family in Washington, DC, and Erik Eagleman's Urban Arrow is still a common sight on the streets of Madison, Wisconsin, ten years later. They have each seen an increase in cargo bikes at school pickups and drop-offs and at the grocery store. While there is no data on cargo bicycling, as of 2020, 5 percent of commuters in each of these two cities were doing so by bike,[31] compared with 1 percent nationally, 1 percent in Atlanta, 2 percent in Denver, and 4 percent in Minneapolis.[32] As early adopters, they are playing a vital role in moving cargo bikes into the mainstream, adding to the army of new bike advocates who discovered cycling during the pandemic or started riding an e-bike for transportation.

I reconnected with Kari Anne from Whee! bikes a year after our first meeting. She told me that the success of her business model, long-term leasing of cargo bikes to families, depends on a specific set of circumstances. There needs to be a certain density of urban families and places that are within a bikeable distance. Cargo bikes can fill the gap for urban families who need a better, more flexible option than public transit. A bicycle culture like that in Amsterdam or Copenhagen, however, is not required. Giving families an option to remain in the city and not flee to the suburbs breaks a vicious generational cycle of auto dependence, but this model comes long after early adopters have spread the cargo bike lifestyle.

The bottom line is that the e-cargo bike is a flexible tool whose uses continue to expand. Its functionality certainly isn't limited to Amsterdam or Oslo.

4

Micromobility: Smaller, Cheaper, and More Fun than Cars

In the fall of 2017, in the "move fast and break things" style the world has grown accustomed to from tech companies, Bird scooters—shared dockless electric scooters—invaded the streets of Santa Monica, California, almost overnight. This was the first wave of shared dockless electric scooters—e-scooters—in an American city, and local officials were completely in the dark. With all the hubris the world has come to expect from tech bros, the only warning of the scooter invasion came after the fact. The *Washington Post* reported that Bird's chief executive sent the mayor of Santa Monica a LinkedIn message introducing him to an "exciting new mobility strategy for Santa Monica" after the e-scooters had arrived.[1]

Narratives of invasion, crisis, defense, and retreat are not new to the transportation world. Long before e-scooters invaded sunny California streets, bicycles were causing terror, panic, and moral outrage. In 1897, the *Columbus (Ohio) Dispatch* reported[2] that speeding cyclists, labeled "scorchers,"[3] were scaring drivers off streets—more than a century before such riders were called "scofflaw cyclists."[4] Nineteenth-century Victorian pseudoscience spurred misogynistic rage at the thought of women riding bicycles, the motion of which would lead "innocent girls to ruin and disgrace."[5] For better or worse, the e-scooter is the latest beneficiary of moral panic and outrage.

E-scooters are the most obvious face of the inchoate micromobility ecosystem. "Micromobility" is a broad term that refers to a range of transportation options. Urban mobility advocate Melissa Bruntlett defines micromobility as "basically, everything from a skateboard to a cargobike. . . . As long as it doesn't have a combustion engine and/or doesn't go faster than 45km/h"[6] (about 27 miles per hour). Because micromobility modes collectively represent so many options for transportation, they are critical for reducing our dependence on cars.

War metaphors are obviously problematic and inappropriate, but they continue to be used purposefully to be frightening, divisive, and othering. The "war on drugs" (and its continuing aftermath) may be the most obvious example of the terrible effectiveness of the language of war, particularly in forwarding racially biased agendas.[7] Metaphors of war are also the go-to rhetorical device to support the status quo, which explains their consistent use in discussions of public spaces and changing streets. In the halcyon days before social media took over the world, this type of hyperbole was mostly confined to satire. For example, in 2011, P. J. O'Rourke wrote an op-ed for the *Wall Street Journal* titled "Dear Urban Cyclists: Go Play in Traffic," itself a follow-up to a 1980s op-ed in *Car and Driver* titled "A Cool and Logical Analysis of the Bicycle Menace."

In the past decade, social media has opened the floodgates for angry (often isolated and typically bigoted) cranks demanding a platform.[8] The internet is awash in raging polemics and conspiracy theories. Today, most of us are familiar with Godwin's law, if not by name, then through experience. Mike Godwin, an American writer and lawyer who represented the Electronic Frontier Foundation (a nonprofit organization defending digital privacy and free speech), is credited with identifying a phenomenon in digital discourse. Godwin's law states that as an online discussion gets longer, the probability increases that it will devolve into someone being called Hitler or another Nazi. Transportation, by nature of the fact that it occurs in the public sphere, is a prime target for inflammatory internet rhetoric. Historically, it has been a battle between cars and bikes.

The battle between cars and bikes goes back as far as the invention of the car in the late 1800s.[9] So it is shocking that in the polarized political climate of 2017, for a brief moment everyone seemed to set aside their differences and agree that e-scooters were the enemy. Their sudden appearance in cities felt like an attack on the natural order of things, and they were impossible to ignore. The "ask forgiveness, not permission" approach was repeated widely, globally, and defended by the e-scooter industry as "innovating and disrupting" the status quo.[10] Cities were caught flat-footed and left confused, trying to figure out what to do. Crowds of people, mostly young, were suddenly riding (and then abandoning) e-scooters everywhere and anywhere, occasionally while drunk. The recklessness of both operators and riders has left them with very little goodwill among the general public or policymakers.

Unlike past transportation novelties, like Segways and not-actually-hovering hoverboards, e-scooters appear here to stay. E-scooters, as part of shared dockless systems, operate across the United States and in cities globally. The US Bureau of Transportation Statistics maintains an interactive bikeshare and e-scooter database, and it reported shared e-scooter systems operating in three hundred American cities in 2022.[11]

E-scooters have been resistant to definition, given the many things that could plausibly be called an e-scooter and the rapidly growing marketplace of variations on e-scooters. They are part of a larger trend in new nonautomotive mobility options. The introduction and evolution of e-scooters is occurring at the same time as e-bikes and e-cargo bikes are being developed to carry all manner of freight and people, more and more electric minicars are coming to market, and motorcycles and mopeds are increasingly electrified.

E-scooters have entered cities at the same time as urban transportation is being reframed in increasingly tech-centric ways. The goal for cities today is to be smart cities and connected cities, cities that optimize form and function with new data and technology. Micromobility has been central to this trend.

The latest iteration of the high-tech, smart city worldview involves combining all the data our smartphones send and receive about us (e.g., where we are and what we are doing) with the transportation options that best suit our needs, thereby bundling an entire ecosystem of mobility at our fingertips. This idea, to bundle all potential transportation options into one app or platform, is termed Mobility as a Service (MaaS). This could involve a product ecosystem created by a single company or provider, such as Lime, Uber, or Lyft. There are also examples of private mobility providers partnering with cities through integration with existing transit apps and services. For example, Uber has partnered with transit providers in Boston and Denver.[12]

The potential for MaaS is compelling, but the reality is messy at best. MaaS platforms are difficult to develop and struggle to attract users. Without users, they cannot help people find more sustainable transportation options.[13] There are also equity implications regarding access to MaaS platforms and privacy concerns about the quality and quantity of personal data that private providers would need in order to deliver individualized travel options at any time and anywhere. The consensus from the research is that MaaS is a good idea but requires further refinement and testing, as well as significant regulation and oversight to avoid the potential pitfalls.[14]

MaaS and related services that aim to provide an ecosystem of transport options accessible within a single app are slowly moving closer to reality. The idea that one could seamlessly transition from driving to a train station to heading downtown and hopping on an e-scooter may not yet be a reality, but it depends on having a vast range of transport options for all types of travel in any setting.

The e-scooter is at the vanguard of the new micromobility paradigm. E-scooter systems are cropping up so quickly that it is difficult to keep track. According to a micromobility trade group, at least 626 cities in fifty-three countries had e-scooter systems in 2022.[15] (This included the estimated 300 cities with e-scooters in the United States).[16] The National Association of City Transportation Officials (NACTO) has tracked the growth in micromobility in the United States and reported that in 2019, only two years after their first appearance on US streets, 86 million trips were taken by dockless e-scooters. Despite a 64 percent drop in 2020 (to 33 million annual trips) due to the pandemic, in 2021 e-scooter rides had rebounded to 62.5 million and appeared on track to continue to reach or exceed pre-pandemic levels.[17] For the time being at least, e-scooters are a significant component of urban mobility.

The Battle for the Bike Lane

While the conversation about cities is plagued by war metaphors, the business world thrives on them. In the 1987 movie *Wall Street*, Gordon Gekko (Michael Douglas) tells his protégé Bud Fox (Charlie Sheen) to read *The Art of*

War by Sun Tzu, proclaiming, "every battle is won before it is ever fought."[18] This approach has extended to the bike lane.

While e-scooters offer a fast, convenient, and fun option for short trips in cities, they often operate in places that were neither designed nor intended for them. Because of this, the specifics of e-scooters as a mode have frequently put them in conflict with people riding bikes and walking. Scooters are too fast for the sidewalk and too slow for the vehicle lane. More often than not, scooters end up being ridden in the bike lane.[19]

The advent of e-scooters was seen as an invasion by many bike advocates who were concerned that e-scooters would take over the bike lanes and cause more harm than good in the fight they had long been waging to take back road space from cars.

Bike lanes are often the result of decades of activism and hard-won political battles clawing territory back from oversize vehicle lanes, excessive parking requirements, and aggressive drivers. It is one of the reasons bike-friendly communities are so rare in the United States. Bicycle meccas such as Portland, Oregon; Boulder, Colorado; and Davis, California got that way through the tireless efforts of bicycle advocates going back to the 1960s.[20] Many of those advocates who dedicated so much time and effort to making their communities better for bikes still live there and are, understandably, concerned that e-scooters will wreak havoc in a system they worked so hard to build.

The presence of e-scooters, and the tension between them and bicycles, raises uncomfortable questions in bike-friendly places. Progressive communities with progressive transportation policies are always looking for new ways to improve their transport systems, but after watching the chaotic and unwelcome introduction of e-scooters in places like Santa Monica, many communities went on the defensive. Boulder, for example, chose the path of many other cities and banned shared e-scooters before their arrival. This was to give the city time to decide what, if anything, to do about them from a policy and infrastructure perspective. As of 2021, Boulder had settled on allowing shared dockless e-scooters that are limited to 15 mph and can be operated only in geofenced zones during certain hours.

The global trend among cities seems to be toward increased regulation of all aspects of shared e-scooters. Oslo has instituted strict regulations limiting the use and operation of e-scooters. Only three companies are allowed to operate in the city. The total number of scooters each company can provide is also limited, their speeds are limited to 20 kilometers per hour (kph), or about 12 mph, and fleets must be distributed in different neighborhoods on the basis of percentages (e.g., only 15 percent of a fleet can be in the city center at a given time) to ensure some degree of equitable access. Additionally, no one under the age of twelve is allowed to operate a scooter, those under fifteen must wear a helmet, and those riding with a blood alcohol level of 0.02 percent face fines and can even lose their driver's license. E-scooter riders in Oslo must yield to pedestrians and can be fined for using a cell phone while riding.

But Oslo, Boulder, and most other cities that allow dockless e-scooters allow scooters on sidewalks as well as streets. The rationale is that forcing scooters into streets is more dangerous than allowing them on sidewalks. Despite this tacit understanding by cities that streets are not meeting everyone's needs, there is little appetite for creating new infrastructure dedicated solely to e-scooters.

Scooters versus Bikes

"All warfare is based on deception."
—*Sun Tzu*

Any direct competition between e-scooters and bikes is largely manufactured by those selling private (i.e., nonshared) e-scooters. Their ads read as listicles for the primacy of e-scooters over all bicycles. E-scooter makers (e.g., Apollo[21] and Unagi[22]) often include blogs on their websites about how to choose between bicycles and e-scooters. Äike, an e-scooter startup based in Estonia, says on its website: "Commuting to work on a scooter gives you a feeling of freedom as you overtake cars stuck in traffic or exhausted cyclists. Scooters are not only a clear winner when it comes to eco-friendliness, but also contribute to road safety and comfort. If you are still on the fence between bikes and scooters, we highly recommend you to try out a scooter, and you will surely not regret it."[23]

Behind the marketing-speak, personal e-scooter companies make a few valid points about unmet transportation needs in our cities, particularly where cycling and public transit fall short.

E-scooters are marketed as being cheaper than most bikes and certainly cheaper than most e-bikes. The average e-scooter costs around $300, while the average e-bike costs about $1,000. Scooters also don't require any specialized equipment. In contrast, specialized clothing and equipment are aggressively marketed to cyclists, particularly new cyclists who don't yet know what they do—and do not—need. You can also ride an e-scooter on sidewalks or streets depending on your comfort level, something you are not supposed to do in many cities with a bike or an e-bike.

From a comfort and ergonomics perspective, it can feel much easier to hop on an e-scooter than on a bike. E-scooter websites talk about saddle sores as a thing of past thanks to the rider's upright standing position on an e-scooter. It's a little ridiculous to think that everyone commuting to work by bike is plagued by saddle sores after a ten-minute ride. However, as a former bike-shop employee, I know that new riders often struggle to find equipment that works for them, and their complaints are often not taken seriously; thus, potential new bike riders look elsewhere for a transportation option that works for them.

Companies selling personal e-scooters have an obvious vested interest in sowing division between e-scooters and bicycles of all shapes and sizes, but there is almost no overlap in the Venn diagram of what bikes and e-scooters are good for. Bikes excel at longer distances and are flexible tools that can meet a variety of needs. E-bikes (including e-cargo bikes) are a do-it-all sport utility vehicle replacement: ideal for traversing cities, buying groceries, taking kids to school, and taking longer trips to and from the suburbs. E-bikes are an ideal car replacement for those in the suburbs who want to trim down to a one-car household or for those in the city who need more than what transit and scooters can provide but are unwilling or unable to buy a car. (See chapters 2 and 3.)

E-scooters, just like any other technology, are a tool, not a panacea. Shared or otherwise, e-scooters have clear limitations: they can't carry passengers or cargo, and they do not do well in adverse weather or on dirt or gravel trails. They are best for short trips by individuals who don't need to carry much. It makes sense that they are most popular among younger crowds and in urban areas.

Party Crashers

E-scooters are late arrivals to the car-lite urban mobility party. It's already a tense party, and e-scooters don't seem to be playing nice with the others. E-scooters are seen as "stealing" users from existing nonautomotive modes instead of helping society to reach the greater goal of reducing driving. So far, studies appear to support this, suggesting that e-scooters are being used for short trips in urban areas that would previously have been made on foot, by bike, or by transit.[24]

Thinking about e-scooter use as a potential substitute for other modes is problematic and potentially shortsighted. It's problematic because the idea of neatly substituting a trip by one mode for exactly the same trip by another mode does not reflect the way people behave in reality.[25] For example, if I were riding a bike to work instead of driving a car, I would likely take a different route, leave at a different time, and probably stop at a different place for coffee. A direct comparison is impossible, and thus a counterfactual argument is shortsighted because it limits the way we think about e-scooters. Yes, when people take an e-scooter instead of walking, per trip they are getting less exercise and are using a less sustainable mode. While this might be concerning, it should be taken with a grain of salt. For all the attention e-scooters receive, their impact in any particular place is limited: there are just not that many e-scooters in any given city. So while riders may be choosing e-scooters instead of using other sustainable modes of transportation, the overall effect is likely modest.

There are legitimate concerns about the carbon impacts of e-scooters, specifically shared e-scooter systems: shared e-scooters have limited life spans. They are often vandalized, but more often, they are simply used to the point at which they need to be replaced. This means new batteries and components and waste from old equipment. Indeed, first-generation shared e-scooters often lasted less than a year, but recently the Swedish operation Voi reported that its shared e-scooters now last for five years.[26] E-scooters may be better for the planet than cars, but the latest research suggests that e-bikes and buses are greener options because of the environmental impacts of e-scooter manufacturing.[27] However, the math and the overall impact on city-scale sustainability is fuzzy.[28] These counterfactual arguments are not wrong, but they miss the point: they are losing the forest for the trees.

The forest in this case is an urban mobility transition to car-lite living, and the question is whether e-scooters help or hinder progress toward that end. E-scooters highlight existing limitations in the car-free ecosystem that we should all take note of. The reasons people are choosing e-scooters over walking or taking transit are myriad, and they probably include the convenience and fun of riding an e-scooter. It's unlikely that the exercise e-scooter users "miss" is in any way equivalent to the obesity epidemic, due in large part to automobile reliance and car-centric cities.

People are choosing e-scooters in urban areas because of limitations in public transportation systems. For short trips in urban areas, e-scooters can be the fastest option and the cheapest (after walking). But transit providers need ridership to demonstrate demand for their services as well as to fund those same services. The burden of proof to fund better public transit is high, and the available funding is low. These systemic problems with the US approach to public transit have nothing to do with e-scooters. Regardless of the specific problems e-scooters pose in cities, they are doing a phenomenal job of illustrating the existing problems and limitations in our transportation system.

Shared e-scooters from four different companies (and a shared bicycle, upper left). (Credit: Jörg Fuhrmann [Intermerker], via Wikimedia Commons)

Metaphor versus Reality

"When distance inconvenience sets in, the small, the various and the personal wither away."
—Jane Jacobs

E-scooters are flexible, able to ride on sidewalks and streets. Without clear accommodations for e-scooters in cities, riders tend to shift from one type of infrastructure to another. An e-scooter rider may move from the vehicle lane to the bike lane to the sidewalk and back, blurring established boundaries in our transportation system.[29]

Blurring boundaries in our transportation system sounds exciting and innovative in the abstract, but in practice it is mostly just really annoying for everyone involved. We interact with one another on streets, regardless of mode, on the basis of a combination of traffic laws and social norms resulting in some general expectations for behavior. Deviating from these expected norms causes tension, pitting people against one another. As George Carlin said, "Have you ever noticed that anybody driving slower than you is an idiot, and anyone going faster than you is a maniac?"

For other road users, e-scooter riders are an unpredictable and uninvited nuisance. But dismissing them as annoying belies their potential for cities working to transform how people travel. E-scooters can be convenient, and they can be cheap, but most important, they are fun. One recent study of e-scooter riders in Tempe, Arizona, found that the top three reasons for riding a scooter were speed, convenience, and fun.[30] Another study from Paris, France, confirmed those results, finding that e-scooters riders were motivated by time saving, money saving, and "playfulness."[31]

Riding an e-scooter is an alternative experience that can open people's eyes to the potential of what our cities could be. This type of experience transforms the mundane into a gamelike experience. Scholars at Finland's Centre of Excellence in Game Culture Studies described this as "gamifying the city."[32]

E-scooters are the latest in a long line of tools—including the skateboard and bicycle—to gamify our environments. In so doing, they open us up to the possibility of changing our environments for the better. We can harness this fun new experience of riding an e-scooter to accelerate change on city streets.

By definition, gamifying places makes them more fun. Fun is valuable in itself, but gamification, as a process, does more than add enjoyment to our world. Gamification is an educational process and a precursor to enacting real change. Tactical urbanism and guerrilla gardening—do-it-yourself efforts to effect immediate, from-the-ground-up community change—begin with gamifying space and rethinking its potential. Most of us can't travel the world to experience firsthand life in different places and circumstances. An e-scooter ride, as modest as it sounds in comparison, can work in a similar way on our perceptions of place. We can recalibrate our expectations for urban space through experience. In whatever form it takes, the gamification of urban space is crucial to building the necessary momentum to fundamentally change our cities.

It's easy to forget that cities are settings for the vastness of human experiences. Cities are the backdrop for our daily lives, for interactions both novel and mundane, exciting and introspective: places of evolving form and function that meet today's needs and tomorrow's. But in the rush to create modern, car-centered cities, we have abandoned the value of human experience. We have traded quality for quantity. Our transportation systems are quantified by time and distance rather than by the nature and richness of experience. Transportation planning, modeling, and forecasting are all based on the economic concept of utility, that is, the relative value or worth of one option compared with another.

Transportation planning is founded on the idea that all of us are rational actors making daily transportation decisions aimed at maximizing our utility. In practice, this means that we assume people will always choose the cheapest and fastest transportation option, and therefore all decisions about investing in our cities and transportation systems should be governed by this utilitarian assumption.

The idea that people choose how they travel in order to maximize utility is a narrow and technocratic approach to decision-making that ignores the richness of our daily lives. It's like assuming that people decide what to eat based only on calories. If you built a restaurant menu around that assumption alone, you would end up with one dish (or one ingredient) served in different portion sizes. This is what has happened to transportation in the United States.

The reality of how we choose to travel is endlessly complex and context dependent. It depends on where we live, where we are going, what options we have available to us, what we have to do, who we are traveling with, the weather that day, and our likes and preferences. And that is assuming we are going somewhere. Travel is also an act in itself that doesn't require a purpose or destination.

The idea of travel, or just *movement and experience* in a more abstract sense, as something to be enjoyed irrespective of an origin or destination is inherently difficult to comprehend or quantify. The idea of enjoying a ride around the block, finding a new spot to skate, or wandering the neighborhood is antithetical to transportation planning. Travel for the sake of travel is not a utilitarian act. It cannot be quantified using existing metrics. It is, however, critical to understanding how to improve cities.

In her book *Wanderlust: A History of Walking,* Rebecca Solnit describes how walking—in addition to being the original active mode of transportation—has served a deeper purpose for myriad philosophers and writers, from Whitman and Rousseau to Kierkegaard and Kant. For these thinkers, walking served as a means for "exploring the unpredictable and the incalculable,"[33] not simply as a way to get somewhere.

Solnit is deeply concerned that our narrowing definitions of concepts like transportation indicate that we as a society have lost sight of the meaningful aspects of life, "the unpredictable incidents between official events that add up to a life, the incalculable that gives it value."[34] She warns of a changing world pivoting toward optimization and efficiency: "New timesaving technologies make most workers more productive, not more free, in a world that seems to be accelerating around them. Too, the rhetoric of efficiency around these technologies suggests that what cannot be quantified cannot be valued—that that vast array of pleasures which fall into the category of doing nothing in particular, of woolgathering, cloud-gazing, wandering, window-shopping, are nothing but voids to be filled by something more definite, more productive, or faster paced."[35]

Her book, published in 2000, has proved prescient. In the intervening years, the trends she recognized have only accelerated. Transportation today is about efficiency. Advancements in transportation technology are obsessed with, and justified by, efficiency. Autonomous vehicles are marketed accordingly—they will speed us to our destinations while we multitask; not a moment will be wasted on looking out the window. Similarly, Mobility as a Service companies promise a seamless, multimodal transportation solution—an antidote to slow and inefficient forms of urban travel such as walking and taking the bus.

At first glance, shared dockless e-scooters fit neatly into the technocratic gospel of efficiency, but this is only partly true. Hidden inside the trojan horse of efficiency, e-scooters have the potential to reconnect us to something more sublime, the "incidents between official events" that we have systematically undervalued. While culturally we may have devalued the sublime benefits of walking, younger generations may be discovering for themselves their own modern variation under the guise of novelty and innovation.

E-scooters, and their ability to gamify streets, may be helping new generations rethink the urban experience—at best, facilitating a shift to car-lite cities. E-scooters can do so because there are relatively few barriers to entry. When building consensus and momentum for change, the goal is to reach people where they are at. Skateboarding and cycling each have long-standing diversity and inclusion challenges, and while e-scooters are not perfect, they offer one more option. E-scooters in their current form are suitable only for single, able-bodied adults. But the industry continues to push the boundaries of what an e-scooter is. The hope is that this will increase their usefulness and accessibility, further broadening transportation opportunities, for underserved groups in particular. While the potential is there,[36] nascent research into how e-scooters affect transportation equity finds that women and racial minorities use e-scooters significantly less than do White people in general and men in particular.[37]

The micromobility space is expanding, providing more options for more people and more uses. The distinctions between the current and emerging micromobility modes are dwindling and may eventually become arbitrary. As policymakers waste time deciding what to do about e-scooters, a wave of micromobility options, alongside e-bikes and e-cargo bikes (for individuals, families, and freight), is rising on the sidewalks and in the bike lanes, adding new users to a small slice of street space. NACTO, which publishes one of the most progressive design guidelines in the United States, recommends that urban vehicle lanes be ten feet wide and sidewalks and bike lanes be a minimum of five and six feet wide, respectively. In reality, most American cities follow older federal guidelines for twelve-foot vehicle lanes and often lack bike lanes at all or sidewalks that meet minimum standards of the Americans with Disabilities Act.

The micromobility wave is set to crash onto the street and directly into the vehicle lane. Oslo has dedicated sidewalk space (and some car parking) to shared e-scooter parking.[38] South Korea and Australia are considering piloting dedicated e-scooter lanes on streets.[39] In the meantime, New York City is expanding shared e-scooter services across its boroughs[40] while also allowing cargo bike delivery trucks (operated by companies such as UPS) to use sidewalks to make deliveries.[41] Channeling more and more users into the same spaces will invariably create conflict between groups.

Creating conflicts on sidewalks and in bike lanes is the wrong approach: cities need to be looking beyond the bike lane to redistribute road space for a changing world. If bike lanes and sidewalks are too crowded, then vehicle lanes should be repurposed. There is some evidence that the trend is beginning. Chicago has seen a boom in shared e-scooter ridership, with an estimated 1.5 million trips in 2022,[42] and continues to invest in new bike infrastructure.[43] In response to concerns that e-cargo delivery vehicles would crowd bike lanes, e-cargo delivery bikes have been authorized to use vehicle lanes and car parking spots.[44]

E-scooters may be the most recent arrivals to a crowded micromobility party, but they are making a splash. They are expanding opportunities for people to move quickly and efficiently in cities, including opportunities to connect the first or last mile of a transit trip to home or office. Most important, shared e-scooters are expanding opportunities to experience our cities in new and novel ways, to remove ourselves from behind the windshield of a car and rediscover the places where we live. Regardless of whether they will remain or be replaced by another form of micromobility, they are bringing new users to new opportunities to travel by new modes. These vehicles will be smaller, lighter, cheaper, and more fun than cars.

5

The Urban Bias in Bicycling

DARRELL HUFF INTRODUCED A GENERATION OF AMERICANS to the concept of sampling bias in 1954 in his book *How to Lie with Statistics*.[1] He did so by telling the story of the 1936 presidential election. The *Literary Digest*, a widely respected magazine at the time, had published the results of readers' polls for the previous five presidential elections and had correctly predicted the winner every time.[2] This time, the poll predicted that Alf Landon would win the upcoming presidential election and defeat the incumbent president, Franklin D. Roosevelt, by a landslide. Of course, Roosevelt won easily, and the *Literary Digest* was humiliated.

The problem was that readers polled by the *Literary Digest* did not accurately represent the views of most voters. Huff described how the *Literary Digest*'s sample was biased: "People who could afford telephones and magazine subscriptions in 1936 were not a cross section of voters. Economically they were a special kind of people, a sample biased because it was loaded with what turned out to be Republican voters." Sampling bias is extremely common. It is a type of selection bias in which data collected about an outcome of interest are biased to either over- or underrepresent that outcome.

Just as the *Literary Digest* readers were a biased population, the narrative about bicycling is biased toward urbanism. It is biased toward density, wealth, and progressive politics. It makes sense: denser and more progressive places are where bicycling for transportation is happening in the United States. These are cities that draw inspiration from places like Amsterdam and Copenhagen, themselves large and progressive capital cities. In turn, the places most receptive to re-creating what has been done in Amsterdam and Copenhagen tend to be similar to them; it is a positive-feedback loop with a limited vision. It limits how we think about bicycles. It limits where we think bicycles belong. The visibility of the successes in bicycle urbanism in bigger cities works to convince the millions of Americans who live outside a few major metropolises that bicycles don't apply to them.

The British cosmologist and astrophysicist Martin Rees coined the phrase "absence of evidence is not evidence of absence" in a discussion about the possibility of intelligent life in the universe.[3] It is a statement that forces us to consider the nature of evidence. In an interview, Rees explained it like this: "I don't think it's anything profound. It's within the context of looking for aliens—if we don't see anything, it doesn't mean they're not there. They may be very different from us; they may not be trying to communicate."[4]

The explanation applies to bicycles as well—an urban bias has meant we haven't looked for evidence of their potential beyond big cities, and we may not recognize it when we do see it. The reality, however, is that the bicycle is a useful tool for individual transportation and as a catalyst for change, in communities of all sizes and densities. But it can look very different outside bigger cities.

The purpose of this chapter is to dispel the urban bias myth in cycling, to demonstrate the ways in which the bicycle is already working as an effective change agent in unexpected places and unexpected ways. About 45 percent of Americans live in smaller metropolitan areas (i.e., counties with fewer than one million people) or rural areas.[5] In addition to making up almost half of the US population, those living outside of urban areas have an outsize influence on electoral politics in the United States.[6] For the United States to change in real and lasting ways for the better, we cannot talk only about big cities.

Before I moved to Norway, I lived for five years in Lincoln, Nebraska, researching how bicycling can apply to a part of the country that is more closely associated with cattle, corn, and cars (or trucks). Nebraska is a big state, with a landmass a bit bigger than all of New England, and a small population (about two million people). It is almost certain that more people have heard Bruce Springsteen's 1982 album, *Nebraska*, than have been to Nebraska. As if in confirmation of the stereotype of "flyover country," a derogatory term for places between the East and West Coasts of the United States, Springsteen's *Nebraska* is a sad and foreboding album written by an outsider.

Lincoln has a lot in common with other small and midsize midwestern cities. College football is king. Home prices are orders of magnitude lower than on the coasts, and the people are friendly. Lincoln is home to the Arbor Day Foundation and has an extensive recreational trail network (134 miles in and around Lincoln). The city prides itself on its parks and greenways, with good reason. The unfortunate consequence of having so much high-quality recreational infrastructure, however, is that it reinforces a stereotype

The Nebraska state capitol, Lincoln. (Credit: Jes Slavin)

that riding a bike is only for fun or exercise. And indeed, if you want to get anywhere in Lincoln, the safest and easiest option is almost always to drive.

Lincoln is a progressive city in a conservative state—fighting for progressive values at the local level but stymied by state-level conservative politics. This dynamic reflects nationwide urban/rural political divides. Despite the roadblocks, Lincoln has become home to a burgeoning new form of recreational cycling, gravel riding. At the same time, the city and region are realizing the potential of bicycle tourism—in a variety of forms—to bring money to the farthest reaches of the state and benefit everyone, not just cyclists. What I saw, and what I learned, has implications for every community in the United States that assumes bicycles are irrelevant.

It all starts with community and consensus: building community around cycling as a fun activity by fostering and expanding the myriad ways in which people can get involved. This is best started through recreational cycling, such as friends riding bikes to grab a meal and a beer. A restaurant or bar owner will notice a group that rides up and spends money, especially if it happens more than once. This can start the process of building community acceptance of cycling among those who have not ridden a bike (and maybe never will). Larger, organized events supercharge this process. Participants find community in common interests, and communities find economic benefits in catering to these new groups. Eventually, communities can reach consensus on investing in bicycling to make the most of its potential.

There is also a larger strategic point to undoing the urban bias in bicycling: fixing Washington. Urban/rural divides start at the national level. Affecting national policy, regardless of the issue, requires building majority support that transcends partisan divides. Cycling, and its economic impacts, can help to strengthen communities across party lines. Consensus can build from the local to the national level, removing partisanship from transportation policy. National policies are one of the many reasons why so many European cities, regardless of size, are so much less automobile dependent than the United States.

Most European countries employ a constellation of transportation policies that make owning and operating a car more expensive and difficult than in the United States. In turn, they follow more progressive national land use and development plans—plans that tend to encourage transit-oriented development, mixed uses, and bicycle and pedestrian infrastructure. National policy agendas reflect the goals and desires of a nation's people in a functioning democracy. Undoing the urban bias in cycling means introducing more Americans, in previously overlooked places, to the possibilities for all of our communities to be more than they currently are.

Undoing Urban Bias

For many, it is difficult to imagine bicycles as useful for anything besides exercise outside of a city. When constituents do not see bicycles as a viable form of transportation, policymakers tend to think that the only hope for these places is electric or autonomous vehicles—technologies that maintain the status quo. But that is simply not true. Communities of all shapes and sizes existed before the car. People lived full and complete lives without cars.

The task at hand is to begin weaning ourselves off cars, no matter where we live. It takes a little more vision to see it outside of cities, but bicycles are a versatile tool that can be applied widely. Ultimately, regardless of the size or location of a community, the goals are the same in an increasingly uncertain future. We need local resilience and sustainability; we need equitable systems that allow everyone to live healthy and complete lives. We need to accommodate those who cannot drive owing to age, poverty, or disability, regardless of where they live. Bicycle urbanism can help us reach those goals by shifting our focus from regional travel to supercenters and big-box stores to local travel to the corner or to Main Street. Auto-centric development keeps cities and small towns from reaching that goal.

Car-lite living is possible in more places than most people think. E-bikes and e-cargo bikes can carry people and gear for miles with ease, and they do not require gasoline or insurance. The COVID-19 pandemic has shown us that we can access many goods and services without leaving our homes. The switch to remote work at the start of the pandemic meant that people could forgo long commutes by car and focus on shorter trips in their communities, often by bike or on foot. Remote options have also meant that products and services, such as prescription drugs and remote consultations with a doctor, are accessible in more remote places, further reducing the need to travel by car.

Distance is not necessarily the primary barrier to cycling outside of big cities. Safety, and perceived safety, however, are problems. Most places outside of major metropolitan areas need basic bicycle and pedestrian infrastructure. High-quality infrastructure is essential to make it safe and welcoming for people to leave their cars at home and take a short trip by bike to a local grocery store, shop, or restaurant. This is a challenge in smaller communities, many of which are likely struggling with basic services and do not want to create a political firestorm by investing in bicycling.

E-bikes are ideal for local trips and can help to highlight the need for better infrastructure in small communities, not just in cities. People can travel longer distances more easily by e-bike than by regular bike.[7] This means they can take detours to use recreational trails, and they can experience the benefits of car-lite living firsthand. Cargo bikes, e-cargo bikes, and the expanding ecosystem of micromobility vehicles can all be put to good use in smaller communities and rural places. The process is already happening. In chapter 2 (e-bikes) and chapter 3 (cargo bikes), I talk about the growth in e-bikes that may have implications beyond major metropolitan areas as well as the demonstrated ability of e-cargo bikes for deliveries in small towns.

The popularity of all-terrain vehicles (ATVs, also known as quads or four-wheelers) in rural areas is proof that there is a market for car alternatives. Bigger, more robust and capable cargo and e-cargo bikes are being brought to consumers at the same time as smaller and smaller e-vehicles and minicars are in development.

While the possibilities exist for bicycling beyond big cities, the primary barrier is overcoming the cultural divide around bicycling. Convincing the rest of the world that bicycles can work beyond cities is one thing; convincing residents of all the places outside of big cities that bicycles matter is another. It is understandable that when all the conversations about bicycling focus on what is happening in Europe or in Portland, Oregon, or Washington, DC, the implications are clear: bicycling is only for these places. But that divide is not insurmountable. The places where cities are changing thanks to bicycling have just been doing it longer. The benefits are more obvious and the ever-present political fights easier.

Announcing to a community that what works in the Netherlands will work in the Midwest, or the South, or almost any smaller community in the United States, is a disastrous tactic. People need context, experience, and understanding to see how something they don't ever think about can actually help them out. People need to see how cycling can benefit them directly and how it can be adapted to their community. It is a difficult ask for anyone (I needed to move to Norway to figure it out).

Incremental change does not need to begin with a bang. For communities to realize the benefits from cycling, starting small is fine. That can be friends going for a ride and stopping for lunch in the next town over. It has to begin with individual interactions that can evolve into connections. An occasional ride that stops in the next town can turn into a weekly event in which more people attend and spend money in a town that may have never thought of bicycling as anything other than nuisance. Those connections then lead to consensus over shared goals. That is the process of community change.

Bike Tourism

Bicycle tourism is proving to be an effective strategy for using bicycles to bring dynamic, healthy, and sustainable change to smaller communities. The starting point for bicycle promotion is different when you leave big cities. It can be reduced to a numbers game. There are simply fewer people on bikes, and that means that riding bikes has even more stigma in smaller communities than elsewhere. Addressing the stigma means increasing acceptance in the general population while building ridership among those who may be "interested but concerned" cyclists.[8]

Lincoln has a long history of recreational riding. The cycling community there is very active, but bicycle advocacy has struggled to bring cycling into the mainstream as a viable transportation option for everyone (not just cyclists) and an activity worth supporting for its larger benefits to everyone in the community.

Before my job interview in Lincoln in 2016, I had never been to Nebraska. I had lived on both edges of flyover country but had never been to, or given much thought to, its center. My family had moved from Cleveland, Ohio, to Phoenix, Arizona, when I was in elementary school. Despite being born in Cleveland (the Mistake on the Lake[9]), I too had bought into the flyover country stereotype.

After my interview, I had some time to see the city. At Method Cycles & Craft House, I experienced firsthand the open generosity the Midwest is known for. The owner, Jason Brummels, introduced himself, and we started chatting. After a few minutes, he rolled out a bike and told me I should borrow it for the weekend to see Lincoln on two wheels. No deposit, no identification, no questions. I don't think I even told him my last name.

I started by riding to the local shops. Monkey Wrench Cycles has an incredible collection of vintage mountain bikes. Cycle Works and its sister store, Moose's Tooth Outdoor Company, are, unfortunately, best known for their location on the corner of a notoriously dangerous and busy intersection on the edge of downtown. Their storefront has been hit *at least* three times in the past three years by speeding, drunk, or distracted drivers.

Lincoln is a case study in contradictions. It has friendly and generous people, a low cost of living, a fantastic parks and trails network, and a lively bike scene. It is a comparatively liberal college town and state capital—a blue dot in a sea of rural red districts. But car culture runs deep in the city and the region. You can access parks and trails in minutes by bike, but one of the biggest bike shops in town keeps getting smashed into by cars at an intersection the city has yet to fix. And as cities across the country and around the world are tearing down highways, the Nebraska Department of Transportation just completed an eleven-mile stretch of freeway south of the city. These contradictions are not unique to Lincoln; if change can happen here, it can happen anywhere.

In 2020, I led a study for the Nebraska Department of Transportation examining the economic impacts of bicycle tourism. We studied multiple types of events (not only gravel events) and considered indirect effects from thousands of additional people visiting the state to ride. We found that in 2019, the state saw almost $230 million in revenue from bicycle tourism.

While bigger may be better when it comes to dollars, small events add up. There is a Tuesday Nacho Ride that starts in Lincoln and follows an off-street trail to a bar and restaurant in the neighboring town of Eagle. It draws anywhere from a few dozen to a few hundred riders, depending on the weather. Riders stop in Eagle at Bailey's Local for nachos and drink specials before returning to Lincoln. In our analysis, talking to the restaurant staff and checking mileage from apps such as Strava, we estimated the ride adds about $80,000 to the economy of Eagle each summer. It may not sound like much, but for Bailey's Local and the town of Eagle, it is a game changer. These events are low-key, noncompetitive, and welcoming. They get people out on bikes, but they also get people in places where no one bikes to see a benefit from people on bikes.

Using bicycle events to change minds and improve places has been an effective strategy for urban planners since at least the 1970s. In bigger cities, Ciclovías (also known as open street or Summer Streets events) have been popular since their inception in Colombia in the early 1970s. The COVID-19 pandemic demonstrated the continued success of this approach in cities for a new generation of planners and policymakers (see chapter 1). Around the same time, two writers from the *Des Moines Register* decided to ride bicycles across Iowa, posting dispatches as they went. Since that first ride, it has become an annual event attracting thousands and bringing significant economic benefits to the towns it rolls through. Known as RAGBRAI (Register's Annual Great Bicycle Ride Across Iowa), the event is estimated to generate $365 million annually for the State of Iowa.[10] It has become so popular that attendance is capped at 8,500 riders per year. Today, the RAGBRAI model forms the foundation of noncompetitive fundraising rides nationally.

Gravel Riding in Nebraska

About 75 percent (approximately seventy-two thousand miles) of roads in Nebraska are unpaved.[11] Riding out from downtown Lincoln, you will be on hundreds of miles of uninterrupted gravel in about ten minutes. It's not uncommon to ride for hours and see only a handful of cars, but you do need to watch for the occasional overzealous farm dog. The Lincoln-based Pirate Cycling League, a close-knit group of friends who love to ride bikes, refers to this as the Gravel Seas around Lincoln. The metaphor fits. There are no mountains, but the farmland rolls along like waves, and the wind is a constant. This is where (arguably) the modern gravel riding scene was born, and it is host to the Gravel Worlds cycling event.

Corey Godfrey ("Cornbread" to his friends) founded Gravel Worlds and was one of the originators of the Pirate Cycling League. I'm not sure where or when exactly we first met, but it was most likely on a bike ride. He is active in a number of local and statewide bike advocacy organizations, and he and I served together on the board of BicycLincoln, Lincoln's local advocacy group. We reconnected via Zoom, and he was happy to talk about all things gravel from his home in Lincoln.

The first thing Corey said was that gravel riding is distinct from other cycling disciplines: "Gravel is perfect. It is super-inclusive, and it doesn't take a huge level of technical skill." He had a point. You do not need the suspension systems and body armor necessary to fly down a rocky hill on a mountain bike, and you don't need to be able to perfectly pace other riders in a paceline on the road. You just need to turn the pedals at the speed you are able to ride gravel. Of course, he neglected to mention the dogged determination and immense willpower necessary to do so, across landscapes where you can see where you are going miles before you reach it. Embracing the midwestern ethic of hard work, discipline, and perseverance will take you a long way in appreciating the allure of gravel cycling.

Everyone in gravel riding has an opinion about why it is becoming so popular, but one possibility is space. The Midwest has it, and the coasts don't. By space I mean road space, that is, miles of (gravel) roads with very little car traffic. Access to good places to ride is getting more difficult to come by for many cyclists. Country roads and roads leading to and through natural parks and amenities have always been popular for road cyclists, but they are also popular with drivers, putting the two groups in conflict. In turn, mountain bikers are often driving past road riders to trails crowded with other users.

The conflicts that crowding creates are not between groups of riders, just an outgrowth of a sort of tragedy of the commons in which a lot of distinct user groups want to enjoy the same places at the same times. The problem intensified as remote workers moved to amenity communities during the pandemic. As riders have struggled to find places to ride, and event promoters have found it more difficult to host events on busy roads or popular trails, both groups have found their way to the open roads of flyover country.

The growth in gravel riding did not happen overnight. It has been a slow progression over the past two decades or so. In 2008, Corey organized a gravel ride for a few dozen friends called the Good Life Gravel Adventure (referring to a Nebraska tourism slogan), beginning an annual tradition. In 2010, as a self-effacing nod to flyover country, Corey jokingly renamed it Gravel Worlds, which would be the unofficial Gravel World Championships. To complete the joke, they printed jerseys with the world championship rainbow stripes of the UCI—the Union Cycliste Internationale—the international governing body of sport cycling, based in Switzerland and commonly associated with grand tours and prosecution of doping scandals in Europe.

In 2010, 100 people showed up for that first year of Gravel Worlds. In 2019, Gravel Worlds had 700 racers. In 2022 (after a 2021 cancellation due to the pandemic), over 2,600 registered to attend from around the world. In 2023, there were 2,000 registered riders from all fifty states and fourteen countries. (Corey thinks the drop in riders was likely due to competition from the growing number of gravel events nationally.) Today, the fitness technology and wearables company Garmin is the title sponsor of the event.

Corey recounted how in the early years, riders and industry people from across the country started coming to gravel events in the Midwest. More "coast-centric types" (Corey's words) would find themselves in Lincoln for Gravel Worlds and immediately shift perspectives on flyover country: "Once they realize the freedom and adventure they can have in these smaller cities. So much access. So many options. . . . They are just amazed at what we have here."

The number one rule at Gravel Worlds is "Be Cool" (it's printed on the T-shirts). There is the option to compete for the Worlds title, but the event organizers work hard to focus on building community and giving back. Unique to competitive cycling, the prize purse is made up of donations and the winner gets to decide which charity receives the purse. As part of its larger vision for a gravel community, the Pirate Cycling League also hosts a podcast, a gravel camp for new riders, a winter endurance ride, and weekly group rides out of Lincoln.

Gravel cycling has exploded in popularity in the past decade. In 2022, the *New York Times*[12] and the *Washington Post*[13] both ran stories about the growth of gravel cycling. Gravel events and groups are growing nationally and internationally. About two hundred miles south of Lincoln, in Emporia, Kansas, is the biggest gravel race: Unbound Gravel.[14] From coast to coast, there are now dozens of gravel events and races. For example, *Bicycling* published a bucket list of the top twenty gravel events of 2023.[15]

Internationally, gravel riding is expanding the cycling world and making it more inclusive. The Lakes Gravel Gang in the North of England and the gravELLE Club in Switzerland are geared toward women and nonbinary riders.[16] The UCI now runs an international gravel series and the UCI Gravel World Championships—a serious (and official) counterpoint to Lincoln's original (and much less serious) Gravel Worlds.

Along the way, Corey received a cease and desist letter from the UCI. It wanted the Pirate Cycling League to remove the traditional rainbow stripes of a UCI world champion from the league's Gravel Worlds jerseys. "We apologized, and they were really cool about it and wished us luck with our event," Corey said. The Pirate Cycling League removed the rainbow stripes, and Corey said the UCI never pursued legal action. "We were just a bunch of dumbass hayseeds in flyover country," Corey added with a laugh.

With all the growth in gravel riding *within* cycling, it is easy to lose track of what it means *beyond* cycling. First are the economic impacts. The study I mentioned earlier in the chapter, estimating the economic impacts of bicycling in Nebraska, quantified the impacts of Gravel Worlds. Our analysis showed that the 2019 Gravel Worlds event alone had a total economic impact of over $400,000 for Lincoln (and the surrounding Lancaster County), with 500 attendees. It's easy to assume that the impacts of the 2022 and 2023 events (2,000 or more registered attendees each year) were orders of magnitude greater.

Beyond dollars, gravel riding brings together people who would never talk to one another under normal circumstances. Gravel rides stop in small towns, at gas stations, restaurants, and bars. Riders spend money and connect with locals. Corey described it like this: "Getting people that they don't normally interact with into a small town is a good thing. Bridge some political and cultural gaps and expose them to cycling." A lot of rural towns have been struggling economically and losing population for decades. A small group of riders stopping to buy snacks once per week helps a lot. Scaling up to a few dozen riders, or an event that draws a few hundred people, can make a real difference.

Changing Communities

Rides and events of all sizes, from Gravel Worlds to the Tuesday Nacho Ride, have immediate benefits and impacts for communities that are mostly assumed to be anti-biking. It goes back to Corey's point about breaking down arbitrary culture-war barriers. These events are also proof of concept to support investing in bikes as a means of bringing prosperity and resilience to struggling rural communities. The national Rails-to-Trails Conservancy has been working on a cross-country rail trail, almost six hundred miles of which are through Nebraska.[17] Demonstrating economic benefits of bicycling for small communities is critical to making this and other projects happen.

Just as gravel cycling has exploded, the culture of cycling is changing across Nebraska, and that is leading to community change. Jason Brummels, the former owner of Method Cycles & Craft House, who loaned me a bike on my first visit to Lincoln, is now executive director of the local mountain biking nonprofit THOR (Trails Have Our Respect). THOR has been running a nonprofit youth cycling development program for almost fifteen years. Nebraska DEVO (short for "development") was created to get kids involved in mountain biking and other outdoor activities. The program operates with volunteer coaches in three cities, including Lincoln. And in 2019, the National Interscholastic Cycling Association (NICA) formed a Nebraska league. In 2022, four kids from the Lincoln chapter won Trek Pathfinders Scholarships, a program the Trek Bicycle Corporation created "to bring greater diversity, equity, and inclusion to youth mountain biking by providing people of color with the bikes, gear, and resources they need to overcome historical barriers to the sport."[18]

The City of Lincoln and its parks department have also committed to building an urban mountain bike park. A few years ago, volunteers built a two-mile loop in one of the city's parks, and its popularity (it's often used by the Nebraska DEVO group, among others) convinced the city to invest in bicycling as a feature of city parks. The new park plan includes a two-hundred-acre site, formerly a landfill, dedicated to a multipurpose bike park. There are plans for additional bike tracks to be built in two existing city parks.

Lincoln is changing as a result of increased public interest in and community support for bicycling. I spoke with Jesse Poore, who has worked as an urban planner in Lincoln and across the Midwest for the past two decades. More important, he is a volunteer with the Nebraska league of NICA, and his daughter is a member. Jesse has worked on bicycle and pedestrian planning and advocacy locally and regionally, and he sees the city responding positively to the culture of cycling. As nonprofits have worked hard to encourage cycling for all youths, and bicycle tourism (and gravel events) have demonstrated that bikes make economic sense, the mayor and city council have responded. In 2018, Lincoln drafted its first bike plan for on-street facilities. Since then, the city has opened its first bicycle boulevard and is working on two new downtown bike lanes. In the past five years, the city has implemented scooter and bikeshare systems (the bikeshare system has twenty-one stations, and e-bikes make up 20 percent of the fleet).

What is happening in Lincoln may not make national headlines, but it is progress. It is more than just a step in the right direction: it is building momentum in the right direction. Lincoln may be one of the more recent examples of smaller communities embracing cycling, but it is not the first. In Twin Bridges, Montana, in 2009, locals built a bike camp for cycle tourists midway between the TransAmerica Trail and the Lewis & Clark Bicycle Trail. Over the next few years, cycle tourism sustained and grew local businesses in the town of about 400 people.[19] In Emporia, Kansas (estimated population 24,000), home to the Unbound Gravel race—an event that usually hosts around 1,000 racers—local businesses say they make more on race weekend than on any other day of the year. Before Unbound Gravel, the city's lone bike shop struggled to survive, but Emporia now has three shops and a growing outdoor industry.[20] In 2022, Montana State University's Western Transportation Institute released the results of a study on how small communities nationally are investing successfully in bicycling and walking and making incremental changes that improve their communities for everyone.[21]

But incremental successes in places that few people visit do not get much attention. By their nature, they have modest effects, and it is in our nature to look to the outliers: the brightest stars, the most compelling narratives. We have to be careful of our innate bias because this sampling bias gives us a false understanding of the world. It is why when the *Literary Digest* surveyed only rich people, it learned only that the rich were voting for Alf Landon.

Likely the most famous example of sampling bias is that of World War II bombers. It illustrates how easily sampling bias can be hiding in plain sight, clouding our decision-making. American bombers were being lost at a staggering rate, and something had to be done. The military enlisted the help of academics. The statistician Abraham Wald examined where bombers that returned to base had been shot to decide where to reinforce their armor. Instead of adding more armor to the places the planes were shot, Wald recommended they be reinforced in the places where they were not shot. He recognized bias in his sample—a type of sampling bias called survivorship bias. The only planes in his sample had returned from battle, so obviously they hadn't been hit in critical places, whereas the planes that did not return clearly had been. By recognizing sample bias, Wald realized the planes needed more armor where they had not been hit rather than where they had.

Bicycle urbanism can also become distorted when viewed through a biased lens. If we pay attention only to the brightest stars of bicycle urbanism, we convince ourselves that *only big, progressive coastal cities (and European capitals) can be bicycle cities*. That might be true if your measure of success is Amsterdam and Copenhagen, outliers in so many ways. But doing so ignores the world of alternative versions of success that are already happening. Gravel riding is not a Dutch invention. The Tuesday Nacho Ride didn't start in Denmark. They are homegrown efforts that are using bicycles to improve communities. If we do not expand our definition of success—remove our bias—we will continue to miss what is happening across the United States and why it matters.

Conclusion

The Path to the Bicycle City

"I sing the city."
—N. K. Jemisin, *The City We Became*

IN A SUCCESSFUL BICYCLE CITY, no one needs to ride a bike, but the option is there. Choice is what I am most struck by after moving from the automobile-dependent Midwest to my new home: a neighborhood in Oslo with good transit, sidewalks, and bike lanes. I have a lot of options for getting around. Where I live, a bike is the fastest way (and e-bikes are popular because Oslo is hilly), but I am glad it's not the only option. Given the choice, I like walking. I like taking the bus. I have spent a significant portion of my life riding bikes in the places where I've lived—typically sprawling suburban places, often with little to no bicycle infrastructure, where riding a bike is dangerous. In those places, if I didn't want to drive, my only option was to ride. But living in a place with multiple options *in addition to* riding a bike is a new and exciting experience for me. The goal of making cities better with bicycles, not only for bicycles, is choice. The challenge is getting there.

There's no time like the present. A constellation of forces at play in communities across the United States demonstrates the potential for change: the pandemic bike boom, the advent of e-bikes, e-cargo bikes, and micromobility.

This book is an effort to chronicle the events, understand the forces, and chart a course forward.

We have seen that our city streets and urban environments can be altered, temporarily or permanently, in a matter of hours to meet our evolving needs. Pandemic street experiments are a helpful reminder that the public realm, the space between buildings, belongs to the public. That space can and should serve everyone.

Bike infrastructure in Hoboken, New Jersey. (Credit: Gregory Francese)

The lasting effects of the coronavirus pandemic on cities remain unclear, but the possibilities are evident, including dramatic reductions in vehicle traffic, equally dramatic increases in bicycling, street experiments, and remote work. At a minimum, these events have changed what we thought possible in our cities, for better or worse. But the hope is that we can learn and evolve, that we can improve the places where we live and work.

As the early days of the pandemic fade further into the background, remote work is one of the few trends that has remained. At this writing, three years from the start of the pandemic, an estimated 27 percent of the workforce continues to work remotely at least part-time[1] as media attention remains fixated on the implications of remote work for downtowns. The shift to remote work for office workers decoupled the traditional relationship between downtowns and suburbs, changing people's daily lives and leaving the future of downtowns uncertain. At the same time, more businesses are doing whatever they can to entice (or coerce) their workforce back to the office. As individual industries and businesses sort out their preferred futures for work, downtowns should not sit idly by.

The pandemic hastened the decline of many downtowns. The state of downtowns today has been described as a "downtown death spiral"[2] or an "urban doom loop."[3] But the reality is that downtowns are overflowing with potential. They will decline only if we refuse to repurpose them. Downtowns are perfectly placed, geographically and economically, for reinvention. Cities need affordable housing, and people want to live centrally and have the opportunity to conduct their lives without being tethered to their cars. Downtowns can meet those needs.

The advent of e-bikes (including e-cargo bikes) has spurred a sea change in how people think about and use bicycles. A viable car replacement is now within reach for more people than ever. The hope is that all of the people who dusted off their old bicycles during the pandemic have been thinking about riding more since those days. Potentially, the benefits of an e-bike can be enough for many of them to act on that desire, becoming early adopters in their communities and leading the way to community change.

E-bikes could be a game changer, but it is not guaranteed. Cost is the first barrier. It bears repeating that e-bikes are expensive only when compared with standard bicycles. They are cheap compared with cars, even used cars. The price of an e-bike or e-cargo bike is prohibitive for many, but treating them as transportation will go a long way toward changing their actual and perceived costs. Incentive programs such as rebates, tax breaks, and vouchers help, but today these are generally available only at the local level, limiting their impact on overall e-bike sales.[4] We need policy change at the federal level.

The nascent e-bike industry has seen its share of growing pains. There are concerns about the safety of some direct-to-consumer e-bikes,[5] and stories of battery fires persist. While reporting on the latter lacks detail, the problems seem largely related to low-end batteries that do not meet recognized safety standards. It is also not clear to what extent e-bikes are being blamed for damaged or defective hoverboard or e-scooter batteries.[6] The industry recognizes the problem. In response, the e-bike industry in the United States has been lobbying for federal battery standards akin to those already in place in Europe.[7]

The e-bike industry is also struggling with the competing goals of profitability and sustainability. It is an extension of a long-standing debate in cycling and can be traced back to cycling's roots in the environmental movement of the 1970s. At one extreme, there are those in the bicycle world who see bikes as a tool for achieving sustainability goals. At the other extreme are those who see bicycles as a product—a means to realize profit. The vast majority are somewhere in between.

In the e-bike world, the competing interests of profit and sustainability can be seen today in the right-to-repair debate. The "right to repair"—the idea that if you own something, you should have the right to repair it—is raging within the e-bike industry.[8] Some argue that exempting e-bikes from right to repair is a matter of safety. Others argue that e-bikes cannot be sustainable if they cannot be repaired.[9]

There are valid arguments on either side of the debate; for example, some components (such as batteries) are dangerous for a novice to repair. But that does not mean that the industry cannot standardize parts and components that consumers can repair. The right-to-repair debate is about much more than e-bikes; it extends across home goods, the automotive industry, and tech sectors. Lawmakers in the United States are making their first tentative steps into legislating the issue,[10] and the European Commission is considering right-to-repair proposals as well.[11]

It also bears repeating that e-bikes are not a panacea for our cities. That is particularly true when it comes to addressing systemic inequities in our communities. Underserved and marginalized communities need safe streets and good transit. Systems need to change in order to end racial disparities in policing.[12] An e-bike cannot solve these problems, but e-bikes and bicycle advocacy can become a part of the solution.

So much of the potential of e-bikes rests on fulfilling the promise of building an army of bike-lane advocates. More people on streets means more people understanding the unrealized potential of our streets today. Micromobility platforms can be an ally in these efforts by recruiting more people to the cause. Recruitment for the army of advocates starts with a modest behavior change. If mobility apps can push people to try a shared e-bike or e-scooter, that experience can reshape their perspective on their city. Every first or last mile of a transit trip can be a gateway to advocating for community change. We need to maximize those numbers to effect change. We also need to organize the masses, channeling the energy of an army of advocates into real-world change.

The options for people to get out of their cars continue to expand. At the same time, the private sector is beginning to realize that business as usual is not the best for its bottom line. The world of cargo has not been the same since the pandemic: rapid delivery is no longer a benefit but an expectation. In response, freight and logistics companies have begun to rely on fleets of e-cargo bikes, which can perform the same tasks faster, more efficiently, and more sustainably.

The growing presence of micromobility (alongside e-bikes and e-cargo bikes) serving families and businesses is complicating street space, making it clear that the bike lane is not big enough. Cities need to be taking space from cars to accommodate a more flexible, sustainable, and resilient transportation future.

Bridging the gap between today's automobile dependence and tomorrow's path toward sustainability cannot be confined to only the biggest cities; it must be done everywhere. Communities of all sizes can use bicycles to shift toward sustainability. It starts with recognizing that even though there is an urban bias to bicycling, the bicycle is an important tool for community change anywhere.

Ultimately, big cities and small towns face similar problems at different scales. The biggest barrier is in people's perceptions. For example, despite the perception of greater distances and the need to drive more in small towns and rural places, the data indicate that households with cars are all traveling similar distances regardless of location.[13] Similarly, there is a perception that transit is not viable beyond major metropolitan areas, but this also is not the case. In fact, transit in rural areas and small towns tends to cost less and result in greater benefits to communities than transit investments elsewhere.[14]

The urban bias means we disregard the potential for bicycles as change agents in small towns and rural areas. We instead turn to magical thinking. In urban and rural places, the promise of technology is both especially enticing and obviously hollow. There is very little interest in autonomous vehicles in rural areas because the technology is perceived, rightly so, as untrustworthy.[15] There is also a great deal of concern about the cost and range of electric vehicles.[16] Most important, vehicle electrification ignores the myriad problems with auto dependence beyond the tailpipe. Instead of supporting sustainable urbanism and e-bikes, the federal government is irrationally focused on creating national vehicle-charging infrastructure[17] and electric car incentives.[18]

Shifting from fossil-fueled to electric cars is not a fast answer to the climate crisis. As a world leader in electrification, Norway's experience illustrates how long this process takes and the unintended consequences of vehicle electrification. In Norway today, 80 percent of new cars sold are electric. This is impressive until you look at the timeline. Norway began incentivizing electric vehicles thirty years ago.[19] Worse still, vehicle electrification in Norway has increased inequities in the transport sector while stymieing efforts to reduce auto reliance.[20]

Micromobility, ride-hailing services, and shared mobility also fail to deliver beyond big cities. These services require a minimum population threshold to be viable. Bikeshare and e-scooter share systems in smaller communities tend to work only in places such as college towns. The potential exists for reducing the need to drive. Bicycles, e-bikes, e-cargo bikes, and other personal mobility options can be used for short trips within small communities. Events, businesses, and developers can cater to a broader range of uses and transport options. The potential is there to create livable, bikeable, and walkable town centers. But in the short term, car-lite living is likely the best-case scenario.

Beyond the extreme edge cases of low-density living, the bicycle is a change agent for smaller communities that may not have considered the possibility of reducing auto dependence. Bicycle tourism can bring economic development (and cultural exchange) to small towns. The growing behemoth that is the gravel riding scene is in turn building a culture of bicycling across the Midwest. The change process can be more nuanced in small towns and rural places than in bigger cities. The process is a social one, depending on friends getting out on bikes, building a community, and expanding that community. Incremental change and consensus (not conflict) lead to lasting change. That is how to build an army of bike advocates.

Oslo: A Case Study in Change

Moving to Oslo inspired me to write this book. The degree of positive change in Oslo in the past decade is inspiring. Moreover, it is a proof of concept for US cities. Oslo (and Norway) share some key similarities with the United States, setting aside the obvious cultural, linguistic, and historical differences that go along with any international comparison. Norway is not a large country, but its landscape is rugged and mountainous. As a consequence of geography, a car is usually the best way to get between the dozens of small cities and towns across Norway, and commercial air travel is the fastest way to travel between larger cities.

From central Oslo, you can look up to see the mountains on three sides and the ocean on the fourth. You can get from central Oslo to the forests and mountains that surround the city in less than half an hour by public transit. By bike, you can do so in about fifteen minutes. In the winter, the best way to get to downhill and cross-country skiing is by bus or train. Visually, Oslo is reminiscent of the Pacific Northwest in the United States. Practically, it has a lot of the same ingredients as so many American cities, particularly western cities. It offers close proximity to nature with all the benefits of a dynamic and growing metropolitan area.

Unlike most American cities, Oslo has strict planning policies that preserve natural space around cities and channel development along existing transportation corridors, both transit lines and roadways. Oslo is working hard to find a middle ground between growth and preservation.

In 2015, forces converged to set Oslo on a path to the forefront of sustainable transportation and urbanism. The city set goals that by 2019, it would remove cars from its center, and by 2022, it would reduce direct greenhouse gas emissions by 50 percent. By 2025, it would increase bicycle mode share by 25 percent. By 2030, it would reduce vehicle traffic overall by one-third. And by 2050, it would reduce the city's greenhouse gas emissions to zero. These goals were a direct result of consensus among city staff, the city council, and the mayor to make Oslo a more sustainable and "people-centric" place.[21]

To remove cars from the city center, Oslo launched its Car-Free Livability Program in 2016. It consisted of a series of street redesigns and closures to traffic. Simple additions like benches and planters were made in some places, and playgrounds were built in others. Over the course of four years, a range of measures were tested and refined. In the first two years, vehicle traffic in the area was reduced by 20 percent.[22]

In the years since its inception, Oslo's Car-Free Livability Program has acted as a kind of proof of concept for the rest of the city and for other Norwegian cities. In 2020, Terje Elvsaas, former communications adviser for the program, wrote: "The aim of the Car-Free Livability Program in Oslo is to improve the city environment and increase city life within the inner ring road, using car-free zones as a tool. Fewer than 1,000 people are living in the area, but more than 100,000 travel in and out to work every day. When launched, the extent of the car-free area was considerably larger than other car-free city centers in Europe. These efforts have inspired the nation, and in Norway today, national, county, and municipal plans have stated objectives of zero-growth in traffic volumes or reductions in total traffic volumes."[23]

The fact that so few people live in the center of Oslo but so many people visit helped the experimental nature of the program. People could see and experience potentially dramatic changes to city streets in a somewhat neutral space. In recent years, Oslo has begun to expand its car-free interventions, focusing on underserved communities. Oslo, like many European cities, struggles with affordable housing[24] and expanding the social safety net to an increasingly diverse population.[25] When it comes to car-free livability, this means focusing new projects in Oslo's eastern neighborhoods—areas that were traditionally working-class but in recent years have been home to a majority of the city's recent immigrants and refugee communities. The process of community engagement in these communities is much smoother when residents can visit streets with similar interventions as those being proposed today.

In 2019, after years of slowly reducing traffic deaths, Oslo reached Vision Zero: zero traffic fatalities in a year.[26] Vision Zero—the movement for reducing traffic deaths to zero—has been central to Norwegian traffic policy since the early 2000s. In that time, the number of traffic fatalities consistently fell nationally. Oslo did this with relatively minimal infrastructure investments. Oslo has some great bicycle infrastructure, but it is not a bike paradise like Amsterdam or Copenhagen. Oslo reached zero fatalities by reducing speed limits (less than 20 miles per hour on most streets) and limiting traffic into the city through tolls and limited parking, demonstrating that it doesn't have to cost a lot to make streets safer. The lesson is simple: giving people options other than driving reduces traffic; traffic reductions decrease people's exposure to high-speed traffic; the system becomes safer overall.

Reducing automobile reliance needs to be reframed as providing people with more freedom and more choice. The Norwegian government prioritizes children's independence by supporting their ability to get around using active modes. Kids and families in Oslo have options. Kids can ride their own bike to school one day, be a passenger on their parents' cargo bike the next, ride a scooter, or simply walk (it's also normal to see parents dragging kids to day care on sleds in the winter). To facilitate this, Oslo created what it calls "heart zones"—areas surrounding schools where traffic calming and pedestrian infrastructure are prioritized to ensure children can walk and bike to school safely.[27] Oslo is also the first city in Norway to join the World Health Organization's Global Network for Age-Friendly Cities and Communities,[28] prioritizing transit access for older people, specifically to enable social participation and access to the city's parks and surrounding forests.[29]

In 2019, Oslo received the European Green Capital Award for its efforts to become more sustainable.[30] Norway was an early adopter of electric vehicles, and the majority of cars sold in the country today are EVs. But such technology is responsible for very little of Oslo's success. In fact, during the past fifteen years, city-scale emissions from privately owned cars and vans in Oslo has remained stable[31] as personal EVs have grown to about 25 percent of vehicles in the city (no American city has anywhere near that percentage of EVs), proving that we can't electrify our way to a zero-emission future.

The past decade of change in Oslo is proof of what is possible when forces converge on a common goal. Oslo is trying to balance technological innovations with good urban planning, centered on making the city better for the people who live there. In practice, it is demonstrating that we can transform our cities quickly to meet the challenges of the climate crisis and create safer, more livable, and more equitable cities.

Oslo's shift in policy priorities is inspirational, but it is not unique. Every place where I have lived has the potential to do something similar. And in each of those places, there is a growing consensus among advocates and citizens that our cities can do better. Cities across the United States today are at an inflection point, and the pressure is mounting to change the course in American urbanism. If we choose to do so, change can come fast, and the benefits of doing so are obvious.

Lessons from Europe: A Difference of Degree, Not Kind

Oslo provides a helpful road map for community change, but international comparisons can be tricky. To better understand what US cities can take away from recent European successes in sustainability, I interviewed some experts. I first spoke with Jill Warren, chief executive officer of the European Cyclists' Federation (ECF). The ECF is a nonprofit organization made up of about seventy member groups representing cycling advocacy in countries across Europe and the world.

Jill is originally from the United States but has spent her career in Europe. She told me about the pandemic experience in European cities. As in the United States, it was an accelerant for urban livability, she said: "The pandemic was a catalyst to create more sustainable transport options quickly." Between lockdowns, social distancing, and fears of using public transit, there was the concern that more people would revert to driving cars. To address this, cities rapidly implemented plans for more bicycle and pedestrian infrastructure that (in many cases) they had not yet implemented.

But, Jill added, there were surprising differences between countries. She said that cities in countries with more flexible rules regarding street space tended to do the most. Cities in southern European countries with less rigid regulations, such as Milan and Barcelona, made dramatic changes very quickly, despite not being known as traditional cycling cities. Barcelona has used its momentum from the pandemic to supercharge efforts to return neighborhood streets to people.[32] In Milan, short-term bike infrastructure installed during the pandemic laid the groundwork for a plan to have the most comprehensive network of protected bike lanes in Europe by 2035.[33] In contrast, in some northern European and Scandinavian countries with strict policy processes, there were fewer pandemic street experiments. For example, while Oslo may have been making significant progress in changing how people travel, it was primarily a result of the city's car-free livability program rather than pandemic pressures.

The barriers to bicycle promotion are similar on both sides of the Atlantic. In an example that will sound familiar to most American bike advocates, Jill said that businesses (in countries across Europe) are always worried that removing car parking in favor of bike parking will hurt their bottom line. This is despite the fact that the research clearly demonstrates that bike infrastructure helps businesses.[34] I have heard this same story from advocates in the United States.[35] In a way, it is comforting—a reminder that things are not that different.

If the barriers are the same, then the solutions can be, too. We can follow the example of cities such as Oslo and achieve similar results. To better understand the process of urban change, I reconnected[36] with Norman Garrick, professor emeritus at the University of Connecticut. Norman specializes in using transportation to make more sustainable places from an international perspective. Originally from Kingston, Jamaica, he spent many years in Connecticut and now lives in Zurich, Switzerland, another European city that has made dramatic progress in sustainable transportation.[37]

Norman and I connected online, first chatting about the unseasonably warm fall weather in Oslo and Zurich and the way in which climate anxiety[38] has crept into even these banal moments. I asked him what the United States can learn from other countries and what are the lessons of the past few years for using bicycles to improve our cities.

From Norman's perspective, urban change is not a linear process. It involves intertwined forces operating simultaneously. Providing for multiple modes of travel and prioritizing denser development, enacting policies that promote affordable and equitable communities—Norman said that "all of those things are intertwined. If you think about them in a holistic way, then you might do them correctly from the start."

Places like Zurich and Oslo are "not car-free," Norman said, "but they really are car-lite, and it adds to their vitality." But it has to be done right. Cars are necessary (e.g., for people with mobility challenges), but cities need to provide better options.

This is where bicycle advocacy has had real successes globally. In the United States, bicycling has gone from a fringe issue that cities could ignore to one that most cities realize they need to do something to support. The rapid rise of cycling in Oslo is only about a decade old, and Zurich's story is similar. Norman has seen it: "Ten years ago there was no bike culture in so many cities in Europe, certainly not in Zurich or Oslo. Today it has taken off." The car-lite framework goes a long way toward not alienating those who have no interest in riding a bike.

The Path Forward for American Cities

In 2015 (the same year Oslo elected the city council that would launch its Car-Free Livability Program), climate change denier James Inhofe, Republican senator from Oklahoma and chair of the US Senate Committee on Environment and Public Works, brought a snowball to the Senate floor, proclaiming: "You know what this is? It's a snowball, from outside here. So it's very, very cold out." It was an unseasonably cold day in what, at that point, was the hottest year on record.[39] Inhofe's inability to grasp the difference between climate and weather, offered as irrefutable proof that global warming is not real, exemplified the depth of dysfunction in American politics.

Our problems today are political, not technical.[40] We know what to do to face the climate crisis, to improve where we live and how we live. The evidence is there, the solutions are available, but we struggle to make it happen. It is not that we do not know how to make our streets safer in the United States. We know how to design vibrant, human-centered places. We know how parking requirements[41] and rigid zoning codes[42] kneecap those efforts and that electrifying our cars is a victory for the auto industry, not the planet.[43] We know that autonomous cars are no substitute for good transit.[44] We even know how to move toward true bicycle utopias by just following Dutch[45] and Danish[46] examples. Most important, we know that doing any of these things equates to measurable benefits to our health, the planet, and the economy.

So much political gridlock is manufactured: it is the result of decades of industry lobbying and corporate disinformation.[47] But the facade is cracking. In the years leading up to the pandemic, momentum was growing to finally break through the gridlock. More people are realizing the benefits of progressive policies every day.

During the first year of the pandemic, Dan Baer, at the Carnegie Endowment for International Peace, wrote, "Washington is not dysfunctional because America is divided. America is divided because Washington is dysfunctional."[48] And yet even Washington managed to come together and pass the CARES Act (the Coronavirus Aid, Relief, and Economic Security Act) with nearly unanimous bipartisan support.

Bicycle advocacy needs to take advantage of the momentum for change in our cities. And that momentum is building. It has been for years. But one of the unfortunate side effects of bicycle utopias like Amsterdam and Copenhagen getting all of the attention is that it distracts from victories for communities at home. In 2015, Portland, Oregon, opened Tilikum Crossing, a bridge for bicycles, pedestrians, and cyclists spanning the Willamette River. Before that, in 2009, New York City transformed Times Square into a pedestrian zone.

The history of federal policy regarding walking and bicycling is not well known. Accommodating bicycling and walking has historically been an earmark, or unintended benefit, of larger legislative packages (which are themselves sometimes impossibly complex). It stretches back to the Americans with Disabilities Act (1990), the first legislation to meaningfully affect walking and bicycling. The Americans with Disabilities Act included requirements for basic provisions for accessibility within the public right-of-way. A year later, the Intermodal Surface Transportation Efficiency Act (1991) was passed, which provided funds for rails-to-trails conversions. Most notably, in 2005 the federal government created the Nonmotorized Transportation Pilot

Program, an infusion of about $25 million to each of four communities: Columbia, Missouri; Marin County, California; Minneapolis–Saint Paul, Minnesota; and Sheboygan County, Wisconsin.

Six years after the start of the Nonmotorized Transportation Pilot Program, pedestrian trips increased by over 20 percent and bicycle trips increased by over 50 percent in the funded communities.[49] Marin County used its funds to help build a 1.1-mile bicycle and pedestrian tunnel, the Cal Park Hill Tunnel, in 2010.[50] Minneapolis–Saint Paul used its funds to institutionalize nonmotorized transportation. It created a public works department with staff dedicated to walking and cycling. The strategy paid off: in 2015, it was recognized as the only US city in the top twenty of the Copenhagenize Design Company's world's most bike-friendly cities ranking.[51] We can build on these successes, but we also need to learn from our mistakes.

Old Habits Die Hard

Historically, bike advocacy has often fallen into the trap of assuming that everyone's problems can be solved by putting them on a bike. Too much traffic? Ride a bike. Need to exercise? Ride a bike. Can't afford a car? Ride a bike. It is a simplistic view of the world, and it is rife with assumptions about the decision to ride a bicycle. Assuming that lack of access to a bike is the only barrier to a better life ignores the myriad systemic reasons why riding a bike may not be a viable option. These reasons can be anything from concerns about racial profiling and police violence to challenges in maneuvering through public spaces.[52] This simplified, paternalistic logic is partly to blame for the lack of inclusion or diversity in cycling.

I spoke with tamika l. butler about diversity and biking. At the time, she was executive director of the Los Angeles County Bicycle Coalition (now BikeLA); currently, she is principal and founder of tamika l. butler consulting. She is also a lawyer and consultant on diversity, equity, and inclusion (DEI) initiatives in transportation nationally. In a 2020 article for *Bicycling* titled "Why We Must Talk about Race When We Talk about Bikes," she wrote about her early efforts in bicycle advocacy and how the bicycle advocacy world wants to talk about bikes (and how great they are) at the expense of larger societal problems. Her response was, "Bicycling cannot solve systemic racism in the United States. But systemic racism can't be fixed without tackling it within bicycling."[53]

Talking with tamika three years after she wrote that article, I asked her how she sees e-bikes today. She said, "When you talk to people who have e-bikes, they are a game changer. There has been a cultural shift (among bike advocates). They used to be considered not real biking." But in her DEI work, tamika is also seeing how the excitement about e-bikes is falling into a familiar pattern in bike advocacy. Specifically, getting everyone an e-bike will not make people feel safer on roads that lack infrastructure or change the fact that so many communities lack decent public transit. At worst, e-bikes can become a distraction from the issues that matter.

tamika is also quick to clarify that when e-bikes become a distraction, it is about more than e-bikes: it is indicative of a larger problem in transportation and urban planning. "We fall into these dichotomies. . . . In planning we struggle with doing both-and." We can work to make sure e-bikes are affordable and accessible for everyone who wants one while also recognizing that not everyone does. We can work to make streets safer and more welcoming for people while also ensuring clean and reliable public transport. Doing "both-and" is possible and often involves complementary solutions. She witnessed proof of this process in Los Angeles during the pandemic. "The pandemic demonstrated that city departments that historically are not great at overcoming bureaucracy to work with each other can cut through the red tape, work together, and get things done."

Going Forward

Bicycle advocates have learned hard lessons about what to do and what not to do. The most important lesson is that bike advocacy cannot go it alone. Effective advocacy requires coalition building. It requires identifying and partnering with like-minded groups that have like-minded goals, thereby building broader and more effective coalitions.

The advocacy group PeopleForBikes publishes a list of five strategies for effective bike advocacy, and the first one is to "bring people together." Bringing people together means dispelling the myths that cycling is a niche activity and that the typical bike advocate is a "quirky, condescending elitist—a wealthy, white male who shows up to work or a public meeting clad in spandex."[54] It means instead doing exactly the work that advocates such as tamika l. butler are talking about: building relationships and cultivating partnerships with all members of the community, positioning bicycles as one piece of a larger whole. There is precedence for this; PeopleForBikes points to the work of the Providence Streets Coalition in Providence, Rhode Island, offering community-based mini-grants for a wide range of projects (many unrelated to bikes), as a good example of bringing people together.

Coalition building can happen within a community, bringing together groups. Coalition building also can, and should, happen across organizations that could be within a neighborhood or work on much larger scales (e.g., cities, regions, or nationally). Thinking about bicycles as a piece of a larger whole means also thinking about how investing in bicycles supports the efforts of other groups and in turn supports connecting with those groups. Health advocates, disability advocates, environmental groups, safe streets advocates, and transit and housing advocates all share a common goal with bicycle advocates. That goal is healthy, sustainable, and just communities for everyone. The Centers for Disease Control and Prevention recommends that communities invest in bicycle, pedestrian, and transit infrastructure to support healthy lifestyles.[55] The US Department of Transportation has recognized the environmental benefits of walking and bicycling since the 1990s.[56] The priority today remains transforming knowledge into action. The larger, louder, and more diverse the chorus demanding change, the more effective.

Bringing people together begins with sharing knowledge and starting conversations. This means expanding access to information as well as access to the decision-making process. In the past, engineers, architects, and planners could make decisions with little community involvement. Outreach (i.e., informing the public) and engagement (i.e., eliciting public feedback) are increasingly required, but they are often treated as a box to check rather than a meaningful process. An open house in a high school gymnasium on a Tuesday night that no one attends is not effective engagement or advocacy, but it was the status quo prior to the pandemic. Just as so many jobs shifted online during the pandemic, so did the way community leaders connected with the public.

The pandemic was a trial run for online engagement. For the first time, the public could log in and witness, and even engage in, the messy (and often dull) policy process. Moving the policy process online also made it accessible to more people than ever before, providing an opportunity for cities to make real progress toward more equitable community engagement. But just as it is unclear what remains of pandemic street experiments, the future of online engagement is uncertain. There is no clear accounting of the amount or type of online engagement that communities have employed during or since the pandemic. Accordingly, there is no clear accounting of whether or not online engagement is being used to encourage equity or the illusion of equity.

Providing an online option for engagement is not the same as ensuring that the process or the outcome is equitable.[57] Cities like online outreach and engagement because it is cheap and easy. Posting a link to an online survey is much easier than hosting a town hall or standing on a street corner surveying people. But having an online option does not mean people from underrepresented groups will use it. It also ignores the digital divide between those with access to the internet and those without. The digital divide reflects preexisting inequities in society whereby marginalized and minority populations are more likely to lack internet access.[58] The danger is that simply by providing an online option, cities can claim advances in equity.

For online outreach or engagement to be both effective and more equitable, cities cannot just publish a link to their social media accounts. Cities need to consider how to promote their efforts (e.g., in multiple languages and across multiple platforms), and they cannot forget about those who may not have smartphones or internet access.[59] Thus far, it is not clear that cities are making the effort.[60]

In Oslo, urban change happened after the city began converting streets in the name of car-free livability. In New York City, changes started with the pedestrianization of Times Square. Suddenly, residents could experience ideas put into practice and decide whether they liked the result. The process, using events or temporary street interventions, is associated with the tactical urbanism movement in the United States, but it has its roots in public health, where it is known as event-based behavior change.

The idea is to use an event to break people from their daily habits and provide a fun opportunity to try something new. Bike-to-work day events are a good example of this,[61] and neighborhood "bike buses" to foster active travel to school are popular nationally.[62] The strategy can be traced back to the 1970s and Ciclovía events (see chapter 5). But it is not always about the bike: guerrilla gardeners have been "seed bombing" empty urban spaces for decades,[63] and Park(ing) Day,[64] when people globally repurpose parking spaces, celebrates its twentieth anniversary in 2025.[65]

The pandemic knocked the world out of its daily habits. The goal today is to create new habits. Cities need to maintain momentum and institutionalize the changes that began as pandemic experiments. Effective advocacy needs clear and achievable goals. For rapid urban change, that means integrating the lessons from pandemic street experiments into plans and guidelines. Doing so ensures that any time a street is repaired, repaved, or repainted, it is brought up to a higher and better standard. Such standards need to account for all needs and abilities and prioritize safety and place over speed and traffic. For example, the National Association of City Transportation Officials publishes a series of design guides that have already been adopted by hundreds of cities globally.[66]

Rapid change extends beyond the street. Straightforward changes to zoning and development codes can free us from an auto-dependent future. For example, minimum parking requirements not only encourage sprawl; they also make it harder to build affordable housing or provide public transit.[67] Similarly, our cities can easily densify and diversify in modest but significant ways by relaxing land use codes to allow for more flexible housing and development. Allowing for mixed-use development means providing opportunities for local businesses to open within communities. Allowing accessory dwelling units (a.k.a. "granny flats") increases affordable housing units, office space, or rental income for homeowners and allows for intergenerational living.[68]

The path forward is not uncharted. It is not revolutionary or particularly new. We have the knowledge, and we have the tools. What is new is the timing. Today, cities have the momentum of the bike boom to carry us forward. The bicycle city is a bridge between the car city of the past and the human city of the future. Just as cars drove us out of cities, leaving hollowed-out centers in favor of formless and endless suburbs, bicycles can carry us back.

The transition process to car-lite living will vary from place to place. The outcome will look different in every community. Instead of endlessly repetitive places, we can construct unique and exciting communities that reflect our needs, today and in the future. Bicycles can spur this transition for individuals and communities in cities of any size. If done right, bicycle cities will look different and function differently in every place, and that is the point. We have tried homogeneity, and it has failed miserably. We desperately need original places.

In *The Scarlet Letter*, Nathaniel Hawthorne wrote, "Human nature will not flourish, any more than a potato, if it be planted and replanted for too long a series of generations in the same worn-out soil." Ebenezer Howard used this quote to justify his vision for "garden cities of to-morrow" as "stepping stones to a higher and better form" of cities. Today, we are realizing this promise. Our cities can become stepping stones to the higher and better forms we need them to be.

Greg LeMond said that in bike racing, "it never gets easier, you just get faster," and that is something I am learning from my vantage point here in Oslo. The work is always hard. The technical and political challenges are real. Oslo's successes can be traced back to a single decisive election, and it is always possible for the pendulum to swing the other way. But that is less and less likely as the city's achievements in sustainability also deliver for residents in terms of quality of life. That is the point. Changing trajectory, entering the race to become more sustainable and livable, is the most difficult part. From that point on, it is all about building momentum with each step along the path. We just need to get faster.

EPILOGUE

In the spring of 2022, I was walking from my office to pick up my daughter after school. The walk took me through the vibrant St. Hanshaugen neighborhood—a trendy district in central Oslo characterized by streets lined with shops, restaurants, and historic nineteenth-century buildings painted in bright colors. While waiting to cross the street at a busy intersection at the foot of one of the largest parks in the neighborhood, I saw a truck stopped halfway through the intersection. As I crossed the street, I saw a woman under the truck's wheels, her torso crushed against the asphalt and bleeding as bystanders tried to help. At first, I couldn't make sense of what I saw, but the events leading up to it started to become clear. Moments before I got there, she had been run over while on her bike when the driver of a large truck turned into her path. The scene was chaotic and horrible. First responders were there within minutes, but by then the woman had died.

The crash scene haunts me, and I was only a witness. I cannot begin to imagine how it affected those directly involved. It is hard to write about it, let alone talk about it. It was one of the worst things I have ever seen, and I think about the victim, her family, and everyone else there all the time—even today, more than a year later. I have lost friends to similar circumstances. I have been hit by cars twice myself while riding, but this was not the same.

There was cognitive dissonance—the inability of my brain to square what I saw with what I thought was possible. I remember at the time thinking that this is what happens in the United States, in the places I left. This is not something that happens here in Oslo.

I know that statistically, the likelihood of a being killed while cycling is orders of magnitude higher in any US city than in Oslo—the city that achieved zero traffic deaths in 2019. Emotionally, it is a different story. It's impossible to know a place is *safer* than elsewhere while also knowing that the statistics do not matter to the victim or her family and friends.

As a coping mechanism, I fell back on my work and tried to process my thoughts through the analytical side of my brain. I started this book describing how Oslo is doing everything right: laying mile markers for US cities to follow in its footsteps. Maybe I was wrong? As the adage goes, never meet your heroes . . . and I was willing to concede that maybe I had been a little starstruck by this new city. Processing things analytically meant I needed to collect some data. I needed to understand what happened and find out whether I could learn from the Norwegian response to traffic deaths.

I reached out to Anine Hartmann, an urban planner specializing in walking and cycling in Oslo, to learn about the Norwegian response to traffic fatalities. She began with some background: Norway had prioritized the vision of zero traffic fatalities decades ago,[1] to the point where it is foundational and implicit.[2] This could be seen in the city's response to the cyclist's death. Anine described how the crash would first be investigated by the police and the driver of the truck would be charged with manslaughter.

Separately, the Norwegian national transport agency would investigate the crash in collaboration with the relevant departments of the City of Oslo. The investigation would result in a report detailing the cause of the crash and ways to prevent future crashes at the site. Anine said that the specific intersection where the crash occurred was already slated for redesign and reconstruction in 2024. Findings from the crash investigation report might be incorporated into the redesign efforts.

Anine's description of the Norwegian response to the death of someone walking or riding a bike stands in stark contrast to the way such incidents are handled in the United States.[3] The American approach tends to center on the individuals involved,[4] how a driver or cyclist behaved, whether the cyclist was wearing bright clothing or a helmet, whether alcohol or drugs were involved. In contrast, Norway uses a systems approach, focusing on how to create a system that eliminates the possibility of traffic deaths.[5]

While Norway is not perfect when it comes to traffic safety, the results speak for themselves. Norway has a traffic fatality rate about one-sixth of that in the United States. That is, in 2022, there were 116 traffic deaths in Norway[6] (about 2 per 100,000 people). In that same year, there were nearly 43,000 traffic deaths in the United States[7] (about 12 per 100,000 people). Another way to look at those numbers is that approximately the same number of people die on US streets every day as are killed on Norwegian streets in a year.

Perfection is impossible because it is a static state. In contrast, people and cities are messy, dynamic, and constantly evolving. Perfection is not the point. The point is the process and the continued progress toward creating a system that is always becoming incrementally safer. The point is that Norway has spent the past few decades creating a road system with the number one priority of trying to eliminate traffic deaths.

When we look to cities that appear to be doing everything right, we think of them as the goal—an end point arrived at after we finally take our cities back from cars. By that logic, cities like Amsterdam and Copenhagen and Oslo are winners, right? They have done what, from an American perspective, seems impossible. The reality, however, is that they have not achieved a long-sought goal. Instead, these cities are starting a race that most cities in the United States have not even entered yet—a race that too many US cities do not even think is worth entering.

What I have learned from Oslo as a case study is the importance of systems: systems built on accumulated practical knowledge, that can in turn respond to changing conditions. It matters that systems are in place to work toward a zero-carbon future with zero traffic fatalities. It matters even as cities struggle to meet their targets. For example, Copenhagen made headlines in 2022 for backtracking its ambitious target of carbon neutrality by 2025.[8] Amsterdam and Oslo have each set goals to reduce city-scale emissions by 95 percent by 2050 and 2030, respectively.[9] These are ambitious targets, and it's not clear whether they are achievable. But despite any setbacks, what matters is that these cities are steadily, and measurably, moving toward becoming part of the solution.

Oslo's larger plans for meeting its 2030 goal of reducing city emissions by 95 percent from a 2009 baseline involve sweeping, cross-sectoral efforts at all emission sources. There are sixteen priority areas in Oslo's 2030 climate strategy, including land use and transport, waste and construction, energy, consumption, and governance, "to make it easier for individuals and enterprises to make climate-friendly choices every day."[10]

As a result of Oslo's efforts, people have more choices in how they travel when the car isn't the sole priority of the system. Too often, sustainability is framed in negative terms of "less than": using less than we currently do, having fewer options than we currently do, and so on. But Oslo's multifaceted assault on emissions has had the opposite effect. Businesses are expanding into new sectors, such as clean energy and carbon-neutral construction. Striving toward long-term climate targets means every day is an improvement, an increase in quality of life, in opportunities and choice, compared with the day before.

William Shakespeare wrote, "What's past is prologue." It is spoken at the start of act 2 of *The Tempest*. In the context of the play, the line is used to rationalize a murder. Since Shakespeare's time, the quote has typically been interpreted to have two opposing meanings.[11] It can be an argument for minimizing the past as only setting the stage for the present. Alternatively, it can be used to mean the exact opposite: that the past holds valuable lessons for the future, lessons that we ignore at our own peril. When it comes to the places where we live, ignoring the lessons of the past will doom us to repeat them. To meet the challenges of an uncertain future, it is clear that we need to learn from our past—to create systems that are responsive to knowledge and are able to adapt and evolve. This is how we will make progress toward a brighter future.

NOTES

Preface

1. Amanda Tomlin, "Raising Hell: The Beginner's Guide to Norwegian Black Metal," Routes North Nordic Travel Guide, August 15, 2022, https://www.routesnorth.com/language-and-culture/raising-hell-the-beginners-guide-to-norwegian-black-metal/.
2. Anine Hartmann and Sarah Abel, "How Oslo Achieved Zero Pedestrian and Bicycle Fatalities, and How Others Can Apply What Worked," *TheCityFix* (blog), October 13, 2020, https://thecityfix.com/blog/how-oslo-achieved-zero-pedestrian-and-bicycle-fatalities-and-how-others-can-apply-what-worked/.
3. Niccolò Panozzo, "Why the Positive Buzz and Darling Status of Oslo as a Bicycle-City?," European Cyclists' Federation, April 18, 2019, https://ecf.com/news-and-events/news/why-positive-buzz-and-darling-status-oslo-bicycle-city.
4. Ebenezer Howard, *Garden Cities of To-Morrow: A Peaceful Path to Real Reform* (London: Swan Sonnenschein, 1902).
5. Howard, *Garden Cities of To-Morrow*, 126.
6. Thomas More, *Utopia* (London: Murray, 1869; originally published in Latin in 1516).
7. Cosmin Popan, *Bicycle Utopias: Imagining Fast and Slow Cycling Futures* (London: Routledge, 2019), 53.
8. Ursula K. Le Guin, *The Dispossessed: The Magnificent New Epic of an Ambiguous Utopia*, 1st ed. (New York: Harper & Row, 1974).
9. Daniel P. Jaeckle, "Embodied Anarchy in Ursula K. Le Guin's *The*

Dispossessed," *Utopian Studies* 20, no. 1 (2009): 75–95, http://www.jstor.org/stable/20719930.
10. Jaeckle, "Embodied Anarchy," 80, quoting Le Guin, *The Dispossessed*, 333.
11. Donald F. Theall, "The Art of Social-Science Fiction: The Ambiguous Utopian Dialectics of Ursula K. Le Guin," *Science Fiction Studies* 2, no. 3 (November 1975): 256–64, https://www.jstor.org/stable/4238977.
12. George A. Gonzalez, "*Star Trek*, Utopia, and Pragmatism," in *The Politics of* Star Trek, 31–53 (New York: Palgrave Macmillan, 2015), https://doi.org/10.1057/9781137546326_3.
13. Ashlie Lancaster, "Instantiating Critical Utopia," *Utopian Studies* 11, no. 1 (2000): 109–19, http://www.jstor.org/stable/25702460.
14. Geeta Dayal, "William Gibson on Why Sci-Fi Writers Are (Thankfully) Almost Always Wrong," *Wired*, September 13, 2012, https://www.wired.com/2012/09/interview-with-william-gibson/.
15. Cosmin Popan's *Bicycle Utopias* (see note above) is a good starting point for further reading. For a more detailed review of critical utopias in literature, see Bill Ashcroft, "Critical Utopias," *Textual Practice* 21, no. 3 (2007): 411–31, https://doi.org/10.1080/09502360701529051.

Introduction: The Bicycle City
1. Melody L. Hoffmann, *Bike Lanes Are White Lanes: Bicycle Advocacy and Urban Planning* (Lincoln: University of Nebraska Press, 2016).
2. Nicholas N. Ferenchak and Wesley E. Marshall, "Bicycling Facility Inequalities and the Causality Dilemma with Socioeconomic/Sociodemographic Change," *Transportation Research Part D: Transport and Environment* 97 (August 2021): 102920, https://doi.org/10.1016/j.trd.2021.102920.
3. David Byrne, *Bicycle Diaries* (New York: Penguin Books, 2009), 22, 31.
4. Ming Zhang and Yang Li, "Generational Travel Patterns in the United States: New Insights from Eight National Travel Surveys," *Transportation Research Part A: Policy and Practice* 156 (February 2022): 1–13, https://doi.org/10.1016/j.tra.2021.12.002.
5. J. Richard Kuzmyak and Jennifer Dill, "Walking and Bicycling in the United States: The Who, What, Where, and Why," *TR News* 280 (May–June

2012), https://onlinepubs.trb.org/onlinepubs/trnews/trnews280www.pdf.
6. Ken McLeod, "Where We Ride: Analysis of Bicycle Commuting in American Cities," League of American Bicyclists, 2016, https://bikeleague.org/sites/default/files/LAB_Where_We_Ride_2016.pdf.
7. Michael Andersen, "The Best-Kept Secret of Dutch Biking: The Dutch Hardly Bike at All," PeopleForBikes, accessed January 10, 2024, https://www.peopleforbikes.org/news/best-kept-secret-dutch-biking-dutch-hardly-bike#.
8. Peter Norton, *Autonorama: The Illusory Promise of High-Tech Driving* (Washington, DC: Island Press, 2021).
9. Carlton Reid, "How the Dutch Really Got Their Cycleways," in *Bike Boom: The Unexpected Resurgence of Cycling* (Washington, DC: Island Press, 2017), 179–210.
10. James Thoem, "What Makes Copenhagen the World's Most Bicycle Friendly Capital?," Visit Copenhagen, accessed September 7, 2023, https://www.visitcopenhagen.com/copenhagen/activities/what-makes-copenhagen-worlds-most-bicycle-friendly-capital.
11. Tania Branigan, "China and Cars: A Love Story," *Guardian*, December 14, 2012, https://www.theguardian.com/world/2012/dec/14/china-worlds-biggest-new-car-market.
12. "China Overtakes US as World's Biggest Car Market," *Guardian*, January 8, 2010, https://www.theguardian.com/business/2010/jan/08/china-us-car-sales-overtakes.
13. Qian Jin, "China's Car Sales Accounted for 31% of the World's in 2023," CarNewsChina.com, August 6, 2023, https://carnewschina.com/2023/08/06/chinas-car-sales-accounted-for-31-of-the-world/#:~:text=From%202016%20to%202018%2C%20China%27s,it%20further%20increased%20to%2033%25.
14. Daniel Piatkowski and Wesley E. Marshall, "'New' Versus 'Old' Urbanism: A Comparative Analysis of Travel Behavior in Large-Scale New Urbanist Communities and Older, More Established Neighborhoods in Denver, Colorado," *Urban Design International* 19, no. 3 (2014): 228–45, https://doi.org/10.1057/udi.2013.30.

15. Molly Hurford, "New Research Shows That E-bikes Are Outpacing Electric Cars Sales in the U.S.," *Bicycling*, April 27, 2022, https://www.bicycling.com/news/a39838840/ebikes-are-outpacing-electric-car-sales-in-the-us/.
16. Ryan Stuart, "Fallout from the Pandemic Bike Boom," *Outside Business Journal*, December 19, 2022, https://www.outsideonline.com/business-journal/retailers/fallout-from-the-pandemic-bike-boom/.
17. Ralph Buehler and John Pucher, "COVID-19 Impacts on Cycling, 2019–2020," *Transport Reviews* 41, no. 4 (2021): 393–400, https://doi.org/10.1080/01441647.2021.1914900.
18. "How Bicycling Changed during a Pandemic," PeopleForBikes, accessed September 7, 2023, https://www.peopleforbikes.org/news/how-bicycling-changed-during-a-pandemic.
19. Wesley E. Marshall and Nicholas N. Ferenchak, "Why Cities with High Bicycling Rates Are Safer for All Road Users," *Journal of Transport & Health* 13 (June 2019): 100539, https://doi.org/10.1016/j.jth.2019.03.004.
20. Jan Gehl, *Cities for People* (Washington, DC: Island Press, 2010).
21. I am referring to the definition of sustainability first articulated by the United Nations in 1987 in its report *Our Common Future*. The report is also widely known as the Brundtland Report because it was jointly written by the World Commission on Environment and Development, chaired by Gro Brundtland and generally referred to as the Brundtland Commission. Sustainable development is defined in the report as "development that meets the needs of the present without compromising the ability of future generations to meet their own needs." The report is available at https://sustainabledevelopment.un.org/content/documents/5987 0ur-common-future.pdf, accessed September 7, 2023.
22. Julia Koschinsky and Emily Talen, "Affordable Housing and Walkable Neighborhoods: A National Urban Analysis," *Cityscape* 17, no. 2 (2015): 13–56, http://www.jstor.org/stable/26326939.
23. Simon Sharpe, "Telling the Boiling Frog What He Needs to Know: Why Climate Change Risks Should Be Plotted as Probability over Time," *Geoscience Communication* 2, no. 1 (2019): 95–100, https://doi.org/10.5194/gc-2-95-2019.

24. Andrea Thompson, "This Hot Summer Is One of the Coolest of the Rest of Our Lives," *Scientific American*, August 31, 2022, https://www.scientificamerican.com/article/this-hot-summer-is-one-of-the-coolest-of-the-rest-of-our-lives/.
25. Intergovernmental Panel on Climate Change, "IPCC Sixth Assessment Report: Impacts, Adaptation and Vulnerability," press release, February 28, 2022, https://www.ipcc.ch/report/ar6/wg2/resources/press/press-release.
26. "Our 'Scorched Planet' Is Getting Hotter, and No One Is Immune to Rising Temperatures," National Public Radio, *Fresh Air*, July 12, 2023, https://www.npr.org/2023/07/12/1187038601/our-scorched-planet-is-getting-hotter-and-no-one-is-immune-to-rising-temperature.
27. Kristie Ross, James F. Chmiel, and Thomas Ferkol, "The Impact of the Clean Air Act," *Journal of Pediatrics* 161, no. 5 (November 2012): 781–86, https://doi.org/10.1016/j.jpeds.2012.06.064.
28. "Our 'Scorched Planet.'"
29. United Nations Environment Programme, "Cities and Climate Change," accessed September 7, 2023, https://www.unep.org/explore-topics/resource-efficiency/what-we-do/cities/cities-and-climate-change.
30. Rashawn Ray et al., "Homeownership, Racial Segregation, and Policy Solutions to Racial Wealth Equity," Brookings Institution, September 1, 2021, https://www.brookings.edu/essay/homeownership-racial-segregation-and-policies-for-racial-wealth-equity/.
31. Emma Pierson et al., "A Large-Scale Analysis of Racial Disparities in Police Stops across the United States," *Nature Human Behaviour* 4 (2020): 736–45, https://doi.org/10.1038/s41562-020-0858-1.
32. Sam Levin, "US Police Have Killed Nearly 600 People in Traffic Stops since 2017, Data Shows," *Guardian*, April 21, 2022, https://www.theguardian.com/us-news/2022/apr/21/us-police-violence-traffic-stop-data.
33. Donald C. Shoup, *The High Cost of Free Parking* (London: Routledge, 2011).
34. Intergovernmental Panel on Climate Change, press release 2022/08/PR, February 28, 2022, https://www.ipcc.ch/report/ar6/wg2/resources/press/press-release/.

Chapter 1: The Pandemic and the Bicycle Boom

1. Simon Shuster, "'I Still Can't Believe What I'm Seeing.' What It's Like to Live across the Street from a Temporary Morgue during the Coronavirus Outbreak," *TIME*, March 31, 2020, https://time.com/5812569/covid-19-new-york-morgues/.
2. Michael Kimmelman, "Can City Life Survive Coronavirus?," *New York Times*, March 17, 2020, updated March 22, 2020, https://www.nytimes.com/2020/03/17/world/europe/coronavirus-city-life.html.
3. Emily Badger, "Covid Didn't Kill Cities. Why Was That Prophecy So Alluring?," *New York Times*, July 12, 2021, https://www.nytimes.com/2021/07/12/upshot/covid-cities-predictions-wrong.html; Steven Conn, *Americans against the City: Anti-urbanism in the Twentieth Century* (Oxford: Oxford University Press, 2014).
4. Ed Yong, "How the Pandemic Defeated America: A Virus Has Brought the World's Most Powerful Country to Its Knees," *Atlantic*, September 2020, https://www.theatlantic.com/magazine/archive/2020/09/coronavirus-american-failure/614191/.
5. Centers for Disease Control and Prevention, "COVID Data Tracker," accessed September 8, 2023, https://covid.cdc.gov/covid-data-tracker/#datatracker-home.
6. Usama Bilal et al., "Tracking COVID-19 Inequities across Jurisdictions Represented in the Big Cities Health Coalition (BCHC): The COVID-19 Health Inequities in BCHC Cities Dashboard," *American Journal of Public Health* 112, no. 6 (June 1, 2022): 904–12, https://doi.org/10.2105/AJPH.2021.306708.
7. Jack Rosenthal, "A Terrible Thing to Waste," *New York Times Magazine*, July 31, 2009, https://www.nytimes.com/2009/08/02/magazine/02FOB-onlanguage-t.html.
8. Tongbin Qu et al., "The Disparate Impact of COVID-19 Pandemic on Walking and Biking Behaviors," *Transportation Research Part D: Transportation and Environment* 112 (November 2022): 103494, https://doi.org/10.1016/j.trd.2022.103494.
9. Adele Peters, "COVID Forced Cities to Redesign Their Streets. Now, Some of Those Changes Are Permanent," *Fast Company*, January 2,

2022, https://www.fastcompany.com/90704448/covid-forced-cities-to-redesign-their-streets-now-some-of-those-changes-are-permanent.

10. Peters, "COVID Forced Cities to Redesign Their Streets"; Roger Rudick, "The Return of Oakland's Slow Streets," *Streetsblog SF*, March 1, 2023, https://sf.streetsblog.org/2023/03/01/the-return-of-oaklands-slow-streets.

11. Ralph Buehler and John Pucher, "COVID-19 Impacts on Cycling, 2019–2020," *Transport Reviews* 41, no. 4 (2021): 393–400, https://doi.org/10.1080/01441647.2021.1914900.

12. Lennert Verhulst, Corneel Casier, and Frank Witlox, "Street Experiments and COVID-19: Challenges, Responses, and Systemic Change," *Tijdschrift voor Economische en Sociale Geografie* 114, no. 1 (February 2023): 43–57, https://doi.org/10.1111/tesg.12542.

13. Buehler and Pucher, "COVID-19 Impacts on Cycling."

14. Peters, "COVID Forced Cities to Redesign Their Streets."

15. Rudick, "Return of Oakland's Slow Streets."

16. Reis Thebault, Tim Meko, and Junne Alcantara, "Sorrow and Stamina, Defiance and Despair. It's Been a Year," *Washington Post*, March 11, 2021, https://www.washingtonpost.com/nation/interactive/2021/coronavirus-timeline/.

17. Jianhe Du et al., "COVID-19 Pandemic Impacts on Traffic System Delay, Fuel Consumption, and Emissions," *International Journal of Transportation Science and Technology* 10, no. 2 (June 2021): 184–96, https://doi.org/10.1016/j.ijtst.2020.11.003.

18. Brian D. Taylor, "Rethinking Traffic Congestion," *ACCESS Magazine* 1, no. 21 (October 21, 2002), https://escholarship.org/content/qt2fb4t8wd/qt2fb4t8wd.pdf.

19. Shani Pindek, Winny Shen, and Stephanie Andel, "Finally, Some 'Me Time': A New Theoretical Perspective on the Benefits of Commuting," *Organizational Psychology Review* 13, no. 1 (2023): 44–66, https://doi.org/10.1177/20413866221133669; Anna Nikolaeva et al., "Living without Commuting: Experiences of a Less Mobile Life under COVID-19," *Mobilities* 18, no. 1 (2023): 1–20, https://doi.org/10.1080/17450101.2022.2072231.

20. Matthew Silliman, "Want to Be More Productive? Try a Fake Commute," *Fast Company*, December 7, 2021, https://www.fastcompany.com/90703258/want-to-be-more-productive-try-a-fake-commute.
21. Buehler and Pucher, "COVID-19 Impacts on Cycling."
22. William Roberson, "Bike Sales Get a Big Boost in Perfect Storm of Demand, COVID-19 Recovery, and Ebike Maturity," *Forbes*, May 29, 2020, https://www.forbes.com/sites/billroberson/2020/05/29/bike-sales-geta-big-boost-in-perfect-storm-of-demand-covid-19-recovery-and-ebike-maturity/?sh=191a2b22f919.
23. Buehler and Pucher, "COVID-19 Impacts on Cycling."
24. US Government Accountability Office, "During COVID-19, Road Fatalities Increased and Transit Ridership Dipped," *Watchblog: Following the Federal Dollar*, January 25, 2022, https://www.gao.gov/blog/during-covid-19-road-fatalities-increased-and-transit-ridership-dipped.
25. Md. Ebrahim Shaik and Samsuddin Ahmed, "An Overview of the Impact of COVID-19 on Road Traffic Safety and Travel Behavior," *Transportation Engineering* 9 (September 2022): 100119, https://doi.org/10.1016/j.treng.2022.100119.
26. Sarah A. Seo, *Policing the Open Road: How Cars Transformed American Freedom* (Cambridge, MA: Harvard University Press, 2019).
27. Tiffany Smith, "Fundamentals of the Safe System Approach," Vision Zero Network, March 27, 2023, https://visionzeronetwork.org/fundamentals-of-the-safe-system-approach/.
28. David Zipper, "Why 'Vision Zero' Hit a Wall," Bloomberg CityLab, April 11, 2022, https://www.bloomberg.com/news/features/2022-04-11/-vision-zero-at-a-crossroads-as-us-traffic-death-rise.
29. Wesley E. Marshall, Daniel Piatkowski, and Aaron Johnson, "Scofflaw Bicycling: Illegal but Rational," *Journal of Transport and Land Use* 10, no. 1 (2017), https://doi.org/10.5198/jtlu.2017.871.
30. Daniel P. Piatkowski, Wesley Marshall, and Aaron S. Johnson, "Bicycle Backlash: Qualitative Examination of Aggressive Driver–Bicyclist Interactions," *Transportation Research Record* 2662, no. 1 (2017): 22–30, https://doi.org/10.3141/2662-03.
31. Daniel P. Piatkowski, Wesley Marshall, and Aaron Johnson, "Identifying

Behavioral Norms among Bicyclists in Mixed-Traffic Conditions," *Transportation Research Part F: Traffic Psychology and Behaviour* 46, part A (April 2017): 137–48, https://doi.org/10.1016/j.trf.2017.01.009.
32. Meredith Glaser and Kevin J. Krizek, "Can Street-Focused Emergency Response Measures Trigger a Transition to New Transport Systems? Exploring Evidence and Lessons from 55 US Cities," *Transport Policy* 103 (March 2021): 146–55, https://doi.org/10.1016/j.tranp01.2021.01.015.
33. Mike Lydon and Anthony Garcia, *Tactical Urbanism: Short-Term Action for Long-Term Change* (Washington, DC: Island Press, 2015).
34. Paulo Silva, "Tactical Urbanism: Towards an Evolutionary Cities' Approach?," *Environment and Planning B: Planning and Design* 43, no. 6 (2016): 1040–51, https://doi.org/10.1177/0265813516657340.
35. Natalie Mueller et al., "Changing the Urban Design of Cities for Health: The Superblock Model," *Environment International* 134 (January 2020): 105132, https://doi.org/10.1016/j.envint.2019.105132.
36. Diana Ionescu, "The Car-Free Revolution Continues in Paris," Planetizen, September 22, 2021, https://www.planetizen.com/news/2021/09/114739-car-free-revolution-continues-paris; Henry Grabar, "How Paris Kicked Out the Cars," Slate, March 30, 2023, https://slate.com/business/2023/03/paris-car-ban-bikes-cycling-history-france.html.
37. Georgetown University Center on Education and the Workforce, "Tracking COVID-19 Unemployment and Job Losses," accessed September 12, 2023, https://cew.georgetown.edu/cew-reports/jobtracker/.
38. Bilal et al., "Tracking COVID-19 Inequities."
39. Jino Distasio, "The Demise of the Department Store Heralds a Shift in Downtown Areas," The Conversation, November 1, 2020, https://theconversation.com/the-demise-of-the-department-store-heralds-a-shift-in-downtown-areas-148234; Gary Sands et al., "Planning for Post-Pandemic Downtowns of Mid-Size Urban Areas," *Planning Practice & Research* 37, no. 3 (2022): 393–405, https://doi.org/10.1080/02697459.2021.2016200.
40. Kim Parker, "About a Third of U.S. Workers Who Can Work from Home Now Do So All the Time," Pew Research Center, March 30, 2023,

https://www.pewresearch.org/short-reads/2023/03/30/about-a-third-of-us-workers-who-can-work-from-home-do-so-all-the-time/.

41. Editorial Board, "Downtowns Are Lifeless. It's a Once-in-a-Generation Chance to Revive Them," *Washington Post*, January 19, 2023, https://www.washingtonpost.com/opinions/2023/01/19/downtowns-cities-how-to-revive/.

42. Alex Fitzpatrick and Alice Feng, "Which American Downtowns Are Thriving—and Which Are Struggling," Axios, May 4, 2023, https://www.axios.com/2023/05/04/downtown-recovery.

43. Tracy Hadden Loh and Joanne Kim, "To Recover from COVID-19, Downtowns Must Adapt," Brookings Institution, April 15, 2021, https://www.brookings.edu/research/to-recover-from-covid-19-downtowns-must-adapt/.

44. Sands et al., "Planning for Post-Pandemic Downtowns."

45. Rachel M. Cohen, "The Big, Neglected Problem That Should Be Biden's Top Priority: It's Time to Take On the NIMBYs," Vox, March 1, 2023, https://www.vox.com/policy/23595421/biden-affordable-housing-shortage-supply.

46. Monica Potts and Holly Fuong, "Rents Are Still Higher than before the Pandemic—and Assistance Programs Are Drying Up," FiveThirtyEight, January 9, 2023, https://fivethirtyeight.com/features/rents-are-still-higher-than-before-the-pandemic-and-assistance-programs-are-drying-up/.

47. Angie Basiouny, "What's Going to Happen to All Those Empty Office Buildings?," *Knowledge at Wharton*, February 28, 2022, https://knowledge.wharton.upenn.edu/podcast/knowledge-at-wharton-podcast/whats-going-to-happen-to-all-those-empty-office-buildings/.

48. Rachel Siegel, "How the 'Urban Doom Loop' Could Pose the Next Economic Threat," *Washington Post*, August 28, 2023, https://www.washingtonpost.com/business/2023/08/28/commercial-real-estate-economy-urban-doom-loop/.

49. Sands et al., "Planning for Post-Pandemic Downtowns."

50. Emma Waters, "Converting Vacant Offices to Housing: Challenges and

Opportunities," Bipartisan Policy Center, July 31, 2023, https://bipartisanpolicy.org/explainer/vacant-offices-housing-conversion/.
51. Mae Anderson, Ashraf Khalil, and Michael Casey, "Cities Reviving Downtowns by Converting Offices to Housing," Associated Press News, April 24, 2023, https://apnews.com/article/cities-downtowns-vacant-offices-affordable-housing-pandemic-cc2cd895fd0f186229f-69b74a133eddb; Jon Gorey, "Office-to-Residential Conversions Are on the Rise—What Does That Mean for Cities?," Lincoln Institute of Land Policy, May 16, 2023, https://www.lincolninst.edu/publications/articles/2023-05-office-residential-conversions-are-on-the-rise.
52. Thomas Sanchez et al., *The Right to Transportation: Moving to Equity* (London: Routledge, 2018).
53. American Public Transportation Association, "Public Transportation Facts," accessed September 13, 2023, https://www.apta.com/news-publications/public-transportation-facts/.
54. Glaser and Krizek, "Street-Focused Emergency Response Measures."
55. Kim Parker, Juliana Menasce Horowitz, and Rachel Minkin, "COVID-19 Pandemic Continues to Reshape Work in America," Pew Research Center, February 16, 2022, https://www.pewresearch.org/social-trends/2022/02/16/covid-19-pandemic-continues-to-reshape-work-in-america/.
56. Shaista Noor, Filzah Md. Isa, and Faizan Farid Mazhar, "Online Teaching Practices during the COVID-19 Pandemic," *Educational Process: International Journal* 9, no. 3 (2020): 169–84, https://eric.ed.gov/?id=EJ1280329.
57. Elham Monaghesh and Alireza Hajizadeh, "The Role of Telehealth during COVID-19 Outbreak: A Systematic Review Based on Current Evidence," *BMC Public Health* 20, no. 1193 (August 1, 2020), https://doi.org/10.1186/s12889-020-09301-4.
58. Logan Manikam et al., "Online Community Engagement in Response to COVID-19 Pandemic," *Health Expectations* 24, no. 2 (April 2021): 728–30, https://doi.org/10.1111/hex.13194; Don Nutbeam, "The Vital Role of Meaningful Community Engagement in Responding to the

COVID-19 Pandemic," *Public Health Research and Practice* 31, no. 1 (March 2021): e3112101, https://doi.org/10.17061/phrp3112101.
59. Nicole Armos, "Accessible Online Engagement in the Age of COVID-19," Morris J. Wosk Centre for Dialogue, Simon Fraser University, accessed September 12, 2023, https://www.sfu.ca/dialogue/resources/public-participation-and-government-decision-making/beyond-inclusion/accessible-online-engagement-in-the-age-of-covid-19.html.

Chapter 2: E-Bikes: Changing the Game

1. ReportLinker, "E-Bike Market—Growth, Trends, COVID-19 Impact, and Forecast (2022–2027)," December 15, 2022, https://www.globenewswire.com/news-release/2022/12/15/2574554/0/en/E-bike-Market-Growth-Trends-COVID-19-Impact-and-Forecast-2022-2027.html.
2. Tony Ho Tran, "Forget Tesla and Electric Cars. E-Bikes Are the Future of Transportation," Daily Beast, February 3, 2023, updated February 4, 2023, https://www.thedailybeast.com/forget-tesla-and-electric-cars-e-bikes-are-the-future-of-transportation.
3. Chris Nolte, owner of Propel Bikes, who has built a following on YouTube for his e-bike (and e-cargo bike) advocacy, made a video dedicated to the growth of e-bikes and e-cargo bikes specifically for those with disabilities: https://www.youtube.com/watch?v=PCcmbdKibA8.
4. US Department of Energy, Office of Energy Efficiency and Renewable Energy, Vehicle Technologies Office, "More than Half of All Daily Trips Were Less than Three Miles in 2021," Fact of the Week #1230, March 21, 2022, https://www.energy.gov/eere/vehicles/articles/fotw-1230-march-21-2022-more-half-all-daily-trips-were-less-three-miles-2021.
5. Alberto Castro et al., "Physical Activity of Electric Bicycle Users Compared to Conventional Bicycle Users and Non-Cyclists: Insights Based on Health and Transport Data from an Online Survey in Seven European Cities," *Transportation Research Interdisciplinary Perspectives* 1 (June 2019): 100017, https://doi.org/10.1016/j.trip.2019.100017.
6. Christopher Mims, "The Hottest New Car on the Market Is an E-Bike," *Wall Street Journal*, September 28, 2022, https://www.wsj.com/story/the-hottest-new-car-on-the-market-is-an-e-bike-2c495e19.

7. Evelo Electric Bicycles, "A Survey of U.S. Electric Bike Owners and Interested Consumers," *Industry News* (blog), September 3, 2020, https://evelo.com/blogs/learn/a-survey-of-u-s-electric-bike-owners-and-interested-consumers.
8. John MacArthur et al., "A North American Survey of Electric Bicycle Owners," NITC-RR-1041 (Portland, OR: Transportation Research and Education Center, 2018), https://doi.org/10.15760/trec.197; John MacArthur, Jennifer Dill, and Mark Person, "Electric Bikes in North America: Results of an Online Survey," *Transportation Research Record* 2468, no. 1 (2014): 123–30, https://doi.org/10.3141/2468-14.
9. Mathijs de Haas et al., "E-Bike User Groups and Substitution Effects: Evidence from Longitudinal Travel Data in the Netherlands," *Transportation* 49 (2022): 815–40, https://doi.org/10.1007/s11116-021-10195-3.
10. Alexander Bigazzi and Kevin Wong, "Electric Bicycle Mode Substitution for Driving, Public Transit, Conventional Cycling, and Walking," *Transportation Research Part D: Transport and Environment* 85 (August 2020): 102412, https://doi.org/10.1016/j.trd.2020.102412.
11. David Zipper, "How E-Bike Rebates Will Make Cycling Safer," Bloomberg CityLab, February 9, 2023, https://www.bloomberg.com/news/articles/2023-02-09/denver-s-e-bike-rebate-program-has-a-hidden-power.
12. Micah Toll, "Electric Bicycle Sales Are Growing 16x Faster than General Cycling. Here's Why," Electrek, October 5, 2021, https://electrek.co/2021/10/05/electric-bicycle-sales-are-growing16x-higher-than-general-cycling-heres-why/.
13. Mark Sutton, "Electric Bike Experts: Which Demographics Are the Customers of the Future?," *Cycling Industry News*, July 14, 2017, https://cyclingindustry.news/electric-bike-experts-which-demographics-are-the-customers-of-the-future/.
14. Castro et al., "Physical Activity of Electric Bicycle Users."
15. Mozhdeh Hashemzadeh et al., "Transtheoretical Model of Health Behavioral Change: A Systematic Review," *Iranian Journal of Nursing and Midwifery Research* 24, no. 2 (March–April 2019): 83–90, https://doi.org/10.4103/ijnmr.IJNMR_94_17.
16. Destinie, "Electrification in Shared Micromobility & Beyond," North

American Bikeshare & Scootershare Association, June 23, 2022, https://nabsa.net/2022/06/23/electrification/.
17. North American Bikeshare & Scootershare Association, "Shared Micromobility State of the Industry Report," August 10, 2022, https://nabsa.net/about/industry/.
18. Transportation Research and Education Center at Portland State University, "E-Bike Incentive Programs in North America: New Online Tracker," January 19, 2022, https://trec.pdx.edu/news/e-bike-incentive-programs-north-america-new-online-tracker.
19. Sam Brasch, "Denver's E-Bike Rebates Are Already Gaining Traction with Residents," Denverite, May 6, 2022, https://denverite.com/2022/05/06/denvers-e-bike-rebates-are-already-gaining-traction-with-residents/.
20. David Zipper, "How E-Bike Rebates Will Make Cycling Safer," Bloomberg CityLab, February 9, 2023, https://www.bloomberg.com/news/articles/2023-02-09/denver-s-e-bike-rebate-program-has-a-hidden-power.
21. Peter D. Norton, *Fighting Traffic: The Dawn of the Motor Age in the American City* (Cambridge, MA: MIT Press, 2008).
22. European Transport Safety Council, "Do Electric Cars Crash More Frequently than Conventionally-Powered Cars?," September 2, 2022, https://etsc.eu/do-electric-cars-crash-more-frequently-than-conventionally-powered-cars/.
23. Douglas Broom, "The Dirty Secret of Electric Vehicles," World Economic Forum, March 27, 2019, https://www.weforum.org/agenda/2019/03/the-dirty-secret-of-electric-vehicles/.
24. Robin McKie, "Child Labour, Toxic Leaks: The Price We Could Pay for a Greener Future," *Guardian*, January 3, 2021, https://www.theguardian.com/environment/2021/jan/03/child-labour-toxic-leaks-the-price-we-could-pay-for-a-greener-future.
25. Molly Hurford, "New Research Shows That E-Bikes Are Outpacing Electric Cars Sales in the U.S.," *Bicycling*, April 27, 2022, https://www.bicycling.com/news/a39838840/ebikes-are-outpacing-electric-car-sales-in-the-us/.

Chapter 3: Cargo Bikes: Big, Slow, and Revolutionary

1. Adam Hill, "'For a City to be Loveable, the Car Has to Be a Guest':

EmpowerWISM Winner Kari Anne Solfjeld Eid," *ITS International*, March 1, 2023, https://www.itsinternational.com/feature/city-be-love able-car-has-be-guest-empowerwism-winner-kari-anne-solfjeld-eid.
2. Daniel P. Piatkowski, "Exploring Support for and Solutions to Family CABs (Chauffeur-Associated Burdens)," *Transportation Research Record* 2674, no. 10 (2020): 874–85, https://doi.org/10.1177/0361198120939963.
3. Laurel Wamsley, "Young Families Continued to Leave Cities Last Year— but at a Slower Pace," National Public Radio, July 9, 2023, https://www.npr.org/2023/07/09/1186483034/family-exodus-cities-census-data.
4. AARP Livable Communities, "New, Free Publication: *AARP Bike Audit Tool Kit*," https://www.aarp.org/livable-communities/.
5. 8–80 Cities, "About Us," accessed September 14, 2023, https://www.880cities.org/about-8-80-cities/.
6. World Health Organization, "The WHO Age-Friendly Cities Framework," accessed September 14, 2023, https://extranet.who.int/agefriendlyworld/age-friendly-cities-framework/.
7. Elaine Glusac, "Farther, Faster, and No Sweat: Bike-Sharing and the E-Bike Boom," *New York Times*, March 2, 2021, updated October 12, 2021, https://www.nytimes.com/2021/03/02/travel/ebikes-bike-sharing-us.html.
8. Kendra Hurley, "The Smallest New Yorkers Join the Pandemic Bike Surge," *New York Times*, April 15, 2022, https://www.nytimes.com/2022/04/15/nyregion/electric-bicycle-new-york-pandemic.html?searchResultPosition=3.
9. Damian Carrington, "Cargo Bikes Deliver Faster and Cleaner than Vans, Study Finds," *Guardian*, August 5, 2021, https://www.theguardian.com/world/2021/aug/05/cargo-bikes-deliver-faster-and-cleaner-than-vans-study-finds.
10. Mark Kirkels, "Short History of the Cargo Bike," International Cargo Bike Festival, ICBF News, September 2016, https://cargobikefestival.com/news/short-history-of-the-cargo-bike/.
11. Kirkels, "Short History of the Cargo Bike."
12. Andrew J. Hawkins, "We Are Living in a Golden Age of Electric Cargo

Bikes," The Verge, March 18, 2023, https://www.theverge.com/2023/3/18/23645151/cargo-ebike-electric-golden-age-prices-utility-dtc.

13. Future Market Insights, "Global Electric Cargo Bike Market Is Estimated to Be Worth US$ 6.2 Billion, Growing at a CAGR of 11.4% by the Year 2033 End," GlobeNewswire, June 5, 2023, https://www.globenewswire.com/en/news-release/2023/06/05/2681959/0/en/Global-Electric-Cargo-Bike-Market-is-estimated-to-be-worth-US-6-2-Billion-growing-at-a-CAGR-of-11-4-by-the-year-2033-end-Future-Market-Insights-Inc.html.

14. Arne Behrensen, "European Cargo Bike Industry Survey: Market Size and Coronavirus Impact," International Cargo Bike Festival, ICBF News, accessed September 14, 2023, https://cargobikefestival.com/news/european-cargo-bike-industry-survey-market-size-and-coronavirus-impact/.

15. Everett M. Rogers, *Diffusion of Innovations*, 5th ed. (New York: Free Press, 2003).

16. Lelac Almagor, "Spotlight on Inclusion!," Bunch Bikes, April 11, 2022, https://bunchbike.com/blogs/the-bunch-blog/how-a-cargo-trike-makes-cycling-accessible-for-children-with-disabilities-or-special-needs.

17. Lisa Stafford, Leonor Vanik, and Lisa K. Bates, "Disability Justice and Urban Planning," *Planning Theory & Practice* 23, no. 1 (2022): 101–42, https://doi.org/10.1080/14649357.2022.2035545.

18. Stafford, Vanik, and Bates, "Disability Justice and Urban Planning."

19. Christopher Reardon, "Disabled Passengers Were Promised Autonomous Vehicles—They're Still Waiting," The Verge, December 20, 2021, https://www.theverge.com/22832657/autonomous-vehicles-disabled-accessible-challenges-design.

20. Laetitia Dablanc, "Urban Logistics and COVID-19," chap. 10 in *Transportation amid Pandemics: Lessons Learned from COVID-19*, edited by Junyi Zhang and Yoshitsugu Hayashi, 131–41 (Amsterdam: Elsevier, 2023), https://doi.org/10.1016/B978-0-323-99770-6.00002-8.

21. Tyler Riordan, Gerhard Hoffstaedter, and Richard Robinson, "Delivery Workers Are Now Essential. They Deserve the Rights of Other Employees," The Conversation, March 29, 2020, https://theconversation.com

/delivery-workers-are-now-essential-they-deserve-the-rights-of-other-employees-134406.
22. William Ralston, "It's Time for Cities to Ditch Delivery Trucks—for Cargo Bikes," *Wired*, September 21, 2022, https://www.wired.co.uk/article/cargo-bikes-greener-quicker.
23. Eva Salinas and Alex Engel, "Online Shopping Boom Fuels Need for New Urban Freight Strategies," National Association of City Transportation Officials, June 17, 2021, https://nacto.org/2021/06/17/online-shopping-boom-fuels-need-for-new-urban-freight-strategies/.
24. Susanne Wrighton and Karl Reiter, "CycleLogistics—Moving Europe Forward!," *Transportation Research Procedia* 12 (2016): 950–58, https://doi.org/10.1016/j.trpr0.2016.02.046.
25. Ecommerce News, "DHL Tests Cargo Bicycles in Germany and the Netherlands," March 3, 2017, https://ecommercenews.eu/dhl-tests-cargo-bicycles-germany-netherlands/.
26. Winnie Hu and Matthew Haag, "Park It, Trucks: Here Come New York's Cargo Bikes," *New York Times*, December 4, 2019, https://www.nytimes.com/2019/12/04/nyregion/nyc-cargo-bikes-delivery.html.
27. Kirian Herbert, "Electric Cargo Bikes Deliver Big," PeopleForBikes, December 15, 2022, https://www.peopleforbikes.org/news/electric-cargo-bikes-deliver-big.
28. Tom Parr, "UPS—Reducing Vehicle Movements with City Centre Container Hubs," Register of Initiatives in Pedal Powered Logistics, September 22, 2017, https://www.rippl.bike/en/rippl-31-ups-reducing-vehicle-movements-with-city-centre-container-hubs/.
29. Herbert, "Electric Cargo Bikes Deliver Big."
30. Bosch, "Bosch Associate Teams with eBike to Help Community Organizations in Chicago," accessed September 15, 2023, https://www.bosch.us/news-and-stories/beth-bond-ebike/.
31. 2020 US Census estimates, accessed September 1, 2023, https://www.census.gov.
32. Ralph Buehler, Denis Teoman, and Brian Shelton, "Promoting Bicycling in Car-Oriented Cities: Lessons from Washington, DC, and Frankfurt

Am Main, Germany," *Urban Science* 5, no. 3 (2021): 58, https://doi.org/10.3390/urbansci5030058.

Chapter 4: Micromobility: Smaller, Cheaper, and More Fun than Cars

1. Noah Smith, "Sudden Appearance of Electric Scooters Irks Santa Monica Officials," *Washington Post*, February 10, 2018, https://www.washingtonpost.com/national/sudden-appearance-of-electric-scooters-irks-santa-monica-officials/2018/02/10/205f6950-0b4f-11e8-95a5-c396801049ef_story.html.
2. Joe Blundo, "Early Bikes Sparked Same Fears in 19th Century That Scooters Do Today," *Columbus (OH) Dispatch*, September 8, 2018, https://eu.dispatch.com/story/lifestyle/2018/09/08/early-bikes-sparked-same-fears/10812113007/.
3. James Longhurst, *Bike Battles: A History of Sharing the American Road* (Seattle: University of Washington Press, 2017).
4. Wesley E. Marshall, Daniel Piatkowski, and Aaron Johnson, "Scofflaw Bicycling: Illegal but Rational," *Journal of Transport and Land Use* 10, no. 1 (2017): 805–36, https://doi.org/10.5198/jtlu.2017.871.
5. Melissa Bopp, Dangaia Sims, and Daniel Piatkowski, *Bicycling for Transportation: An Evidence-Base for Communities* (Amsterdam: Elsevier, 2018).
6. Melissa Bruntlett, "How Electric Cycles and Micro-Mobility Are Enabling More Inclusive Transport," Women Mobilize Women, accessed August 10, 2023, https://womenmobilize.org/how-electric-cycles-and-micro-mobility-are-enabling-more-inclusive-transport-by-melissa-bruntlett/.
7. andré douglas pond cummings and Stephen A. Ramirez, "The Racist Roots of the War on Drugs and the Myth of Equal Protection for People of Color," *University of Arkansas at Little Rock Law Review* 44, no. 4 (2022), https://lawrepository.ualr.edu/lawreview/vol44/iss4/1; Michelle Alexander, *The New Jim Crow: Mass Incarceration in the Age of Colorblindness* (New York: New Press, 2010).
8. Emily Kubin and Christian von Sikorski, "The Role of (Social) Media in Political Polarization: A Systematic Review," *Annals of the International*

Communication Association 45, no. 3 (2021): 188–206, https://doi.org/10.1080/23808985.2021.1976070.
9. Peter D. Norton, *Fighting Traffic: The Dawn of the Motor Age in the American City* (Cambridge, MA: MIT Press, 2008).
10. Chris Bryant, "Is the Electric Scooter Apocalypse Finally upon Us?," *Washington Post*, November 15, 2022, https://www.washingtonpost.com/business/is-the-electric-scooter-apocalypse-finally-upon-us/2022/11/15/8fe78c4e-64b9-11ed-b08c-3ce222607059_story.html.
11. US Department of Transportation, Bureau of Transportation Statistics, "Bikeshare and E-Scooter Systems in the US," updated July 10, 2023, https://data.bts.gov/stories/s/Bikeshare-and-e-scooters-in-the-US-/fwcs-jprj.
12. David Reich, "Partnering with Transit Agencies: Integrating Public Transportation into the Uber App," Uber Newsroom, January 1, 2019, https://www.uber.com/newsroom/publictransit.
13. Anne Durand et al., "Mobility-as-a-Service and Changes in Travel Preferences and Travel Behaviour: A Literature Review," October 2018, https://www.researchgate.net/profile/Anne-Durand-6/publication/330958677_Mobility-as-a-Service_and_changes_in_travel_preferences_and_travel_behaviour_a_literature_review/links/5c5d5bae45851582c3d60c0f/Mobility-as-a-Service-and-changes-in-travel-preferences-and-travel-behaviour-a-literature-review.pdf.
14. Kate Pangbourne et al., "Questioning Mobility as a Service: Unanticipated Implications for Society and Governance," *Transportation Research Part A: Policy and Practice* 131 (January 2020): 35–49, https://doi.org/10.1016/j.tra.2019.09.033.
15. Mobility Makers, "How E-Scooters Will Shape Cities This 2022," accessed September 14, 2023, https://mobilitymakers.co/howe-scooters-will-shape-cities-this-2022/.
16. US Department of Transportation, Bureau of Transportation Statistics, "Bikeshare and E-Scooter Systems in the US."
17. National Association of City Transportation Officials, "Shared Micromobility in the U.S. 2020–2021: Half a Billion Trips on Shared Micromobility since 2010," November 2022, https://nacto.org/wp-content

/uploads/2022/12/2020-2021_shared_micro_snapshot_Dec7_2022.pdf.
18. Jozef Hlavatý and JánLižbetin, "The Use of *The Art of War* Ideas in the Strategic Decision-Making of the Company," *Transportation Research Procedia* 55 (2021): 1273–80, https://doi.org/10.1016/j.trpro.2021.07.110.
19. Wenwen Zhang et al., "What Type of Infrastructures Do E-Scooter Riders Prefer? A Route Choice Model," *Transportation Research Part D: Transport and Environment* 94 (May 2021): 102761, https://doi.org/10.1016/j.trd.2021.102761.
20. Alejandro Henao et al., "Sustainable Transportation Infrastructure Investments and Mode Share Changes: A 20-Year Background of Boulder, Colorado," *Transport Policy* 37 (January 2015): 64–71, https://doi.org/10.1016/j.tranpol.2014.09.012; Ted Buehler and Susan Handy, "Fifty Years of Bicycle Policy in Davis, California," *Transportation Research Record* 2074, no. 1 (2008): 52–57, https://doi.org/10.3141/2074-07.
21. Apollo, "Electric Scooter vs Electric Bike: Which One Should You Get?," April 6, 2023, https://apolloscooters.co/blogs/news/electric-scooter-vs-electric-bike-which-one-should-you-get.
22. Unagi, "Electric Bikes vs Electric Scooters: Which One Should You Choose?," accessed February 5, 2023, https://unagiscooters.com/scooter-articles/electric-bikes-vs-electric-scooters-which-one-should-you-choose/.
23. Äike, "Bike vs. Scooter: The Big Comparison," July 14, 2022, https://rideaike.com/blog/bike-vs-scooter/.
24. Mauricio Orozco-Fontalvo, Luis Llerena, and Victor Cantillo, "Dockless Electric Scooters: A Review of a Growing Micromobility Mode," *International Journal of Sustainable Transportation* 17, no. 4 (2023): 406–22, https://doi.org/10.1080/15568318.2022.2044097.
25. Daniel P. Piatkowski, Kevin J. Krizek, and Susan L. Handy, "Accounting for the Short-Term Substitution Effects of Walking and Cycling in Sustainable Transportation," *Travel Behaviour and Society* 2, no. 1 (January 2015): 32–41, https://doi.org/10.1016/j.tbs.2014.07.004.
26. Sam Phillips, "Voi Survey Shows Car Use Reduced Thanks to Shared-Mobility Solutions," Move Electric, August 25, 2022, https://www.move

electric.com/e-scooters/voi-survey-shows-car-use-reduced-thanks-shared-mobility-solutions.
27. Chris Teale, "Study: E-Scooters More Harmful to Environment than E-Bikes, Some Buses," Smart Cities Dive, August 15, 2019, https://www.smartcitiesdive.com/news/study-e-scooters-more-harmful-to-environment-than-e-bikes-some-buses/560217/.
28. Abubakr Ziedan et al., "Complement or Compete? The Effects of Shared Electric Scooters on Bus Ridership," *Transportation Research Part D: Transport and Environment* 101 (December 2021): 103098, https://doi.org/10.1016/j.trd.2021.103098.
29. Hebe Gibson, Angela Curl, and Lee Thompson, "Blurred Boundaries: E-Scooter Riders' and Pedestrians' Experiences of Sharing Space," *Mobilities* 17, no. 1 (2022): 69–84, https://doi.org/10.1080/17450101.2021.1967097.
30. Rebecca L. Sanders, Michael Branion-Calles, and Trisalyn A. Nelson, "To Scoot or Not to Scoot: Findings from a Recent Survey about the Benefits and Barriers of Using E-Scooters for Riders and Non-Riders," *Transportation Research Part A: Policy and Practice* 139 (September 2020): 217–27, https://doi.org/10.1016/j.tra.2020.07.009.
31. Zoi Christoforou et al., "Who Is Using E-Scooters and How? Evidence from Paris," *Transportation Research Part D: Transport and Environment* 92 (March 2021): 102708, https://doi.org/10.1016/j.trd.2021.102708.
32. Eetu Wallius et al., "Gamifying the City: E-Scooters and the Critical Tensions of Playful Urban Mobility," *Mobilities* 17, no. 1 (2022): 85–101, https://doi.org/10.1080/17450101.2021.1985382.
33. Rebecca Solnit, *Wanderlust: A History of Walking* (New York: Viking, 2000), 10.
34. Solnit, *Wanderlust*, 10.
35. Solnit, *Wanderlust*, 10.
36. Portland State University, "New Tools Can Operationalize Equity in 239 E-Scooter and Bike Share Programs across the U.S.," ScienceDaily, August 12, 2022, https://www.sciencedaily.com/releases/2022/08/220812114022.htm.
37. Michael McQueen and Kelly J. Clifton, "Assessing the Perception of

E-Scooters as a Practical and Equitable First-Mile/Last-Mile Solution," *Transportation Research Part A: Policy and Practice* 165 (November 2022): 395–418, https://doi.org/10.1016/j.tra.2022.09.021.

38. Katrine Karlsen et al., "Summary: Parking Solutions for Shared E-Scooters," Norwegian Centre for Transport Research, Institute of Transport Economics, 2021, https://www.toi.no/getfile.php/1355170-612191904/Publikasjoner/TØI%20rapporter/2021/1821-2021/1821-2020_Summary.pdf.

39. James Norman, "'Bottom of the Food Chain': E-Scooter Riders Push for Reimagining of Australia's Bike Lanes," *Guardian*, September 16, 2023, https://www.theguardian.com/australia-news/2023/sep/17/bottom-of-the-food-chain-australias-e-scooter-users-just-want-a-safe-space-to-ride; Moon Joon-hyun, "E-Scooter-Only Lanes Mulled for Better Safety," *Korea Herald*, August 27, 2023, https://www.koreaherald.com/view.php?ud=20230827000117.

40. Diana Ionescu, "E-Scooters Are Rolling into Queens," Planetizen, June 19, 2023, https://www.planetizen.com/news/2023/06/124021-e-scooters-are-rolling-queens.

41. Carol Tannenhauser, "Rule Change Would Let 'Larger' Electric Cargo Bikes Make Sidewalk Deliveries," West Side Rag, September 8, 2023, https://www.westsiderag.com/2023/09/08/rule-change-would-let-larger-electric-cargo-bikes-make-sidewalk-deliveries-heres-how-to-comment.

42. Patrick Spauster and Cameron Bolton, "Chicago's E-Scooter Program Is Zooming Ahead, but Equity Gaps Remain," Streetsblog Chicago, August 25, 2023, https://chi.streetsblog.org/2023/08/25/chicagos-e-scooter-program-is-zooming-ahead-but-equity-gaps-remain#.

43. Chicago Department of Transportation, "CDOT Releases Updated Cycling Strategy to Expand Bike Network and Increase Everyday Cycling in Chicago," news release, March 29, 2023, https://www.chicago.gov/city/en/depts/cdot/provdrs/bike/news/2023/march/cdot-releases-updated-cycling-strategy-to-expand-bike-network-an.html.

44. Joe Ward, "Delivery E-Bikes Get OK to Use City Streets for Package DropOffs," Block Club Chicago, October 7, 2020, https://blockclub

chicago.org/2020/10/07/delivery-e-bikes-get-ok-to-use-city-streets-for-package-drop-offs/.

Chapter 5: The Urban Bias in Bicycling
1. Darrell Huff, *How to Lie with Statistics* (New York: W. W. Norton, 1954).
2. "Landon in a Landslide: The Poll That Changed Polling," History Matters: The U.S. Survey Course on the Web, accessed June 16, 2023, https://historymatters.gmu.edu/d/5168/.
3. Errol Morris, "The Certainty of Donald Rumsfeld (Part 4)," *New York Times*, March 28, 2014, https://archive.nytimes.com/opinionator.blogs.nytimes.com/2014/03/28/the-certainty-of-donald-rumsfeld-part-4/#more-152504.
4. Morris, "Certainty of Donald Rumsfeld."
5. Richard Fry, "Prior to COVID-19, Urban Core Counties in the U.S. Were Gaining Vitality on Key Measures," Pew Research Center, July 29, 2020, https://www.pewresearch.org/social-trends/2020/07/29/prior-to-covid-19-urban-core-counties-in-the-u-s-were-gaining-vitality-on-key-measures/.
6. Jonathan A. Rodden, *Why Cities Lose: The Deep Roots of the Urban-Rural Political Divide* (New York: Hachette Book Group, 2019).
7. Ziwen Ling et al., "Differences of Cycling Experiences and Perceptions between E-Bike and Bicycle Users in the United States," *Sustainability* 9, no. 9 (2017): 1662, https://doi.org/10.3390/su9091662; Aslak Fyhri and Hanne Beate Sundfør, "Do People Who Buy E-Bikes Cycle More?," *Transportation Research Part D: Transport and Environment* 86 (September 2020): 102422, https://doi.org/10.1016/j.trd.2020.102422.
8. Jennifer Dill and Nathan McNeil, "Four Types of Cyclists? Examination of Typology for Better Understanding of Bicycling Behavior and Potential," *Transportation Research Record* 2387, no. 1 (2013): 129–38, https://doi.org/10.3141/2387-15.
9. J. Mark Souther, "From 'the Mistake on the Lake' to 'Defend Together': The Long (and Amusing) History of Trying to Rebrand Cleveland," *Belt Magazine*, October 3, 2017, https://beltmag.com/mistake-lake-defend-together-long-amusing-history-trying-rebrand-cleveland/#:~:

text=Cleveland%27s%20inner%20city%2C%20like%20that,The%20 Mistake%200n%20the%20Lake.
10. RAGBRAI, "Economic Study Shows Bicycling Generates $364.8 Million Annually for Iowa," January 26, 2012, https://ragbrai.com/tag/economic-impact-of-bicycles/.
11. Richard Wood et al., "Improvement of Low Traffic Volume Gravel Roads in Nebraska," Nebraska Department of Transportation Research Report 3-2020, March 2020, https://digitalcommons.unl.edu/cgi/viewcontent.cgi?article=1245&context=ndor.
12. Hannah Singleton, "Gravel Biking Is Picking Up Speed," *New York Times*, September 14, 2022, https://www.nytimes.com/2022/09/14/well/move/gravel-biking.html.
13. Pam Moore, "What Gravel Cycling Is and Why You Should Give It a Try," *Washington Post*, May 9, 2022, https://www.washingtonpost.com/wellness/2022/05/09/gravel-cycling-primer/.
14. Life Time Unbound Gravel, https://www.unboundgravel.com.
15. Selene Yeager, "20 Best Gravel Rides to Add to Your Bucket List," *Bicycling*, updated October 21, 2022, https://www.bicycling.com/rides/a38013915/best-gravel-bike-races/.
16. Katherine Moore, "How Gravel Is Breaking Down Boundaries with a New Type of Cycling Club," BikeRadar, January 17, 2023, https://www.bikeradar.com/features/longreads/gravel-cycling-clubs/.
17. Rails-to-Trails Conservancy, "Great American Rail-Trail: Nebraska," accessed October 26, 2023, https://www.railstotrails.org/greatamericanrailtrail/route/nebraska/.
18. Nebraska Mountain Bike Trails Project, "Interscholastic Nebraska Cycling League," accessed October 26, 2023, https://nebraskamtb.org/2022/05/13/trek-pathfinder-scholarships-announced/.
19. Caitlin NA Giddings, "How Bike Touring Saved This Small Town," *Bicycling*, February 8, 2016, https://www.bicycling.com/rides/a20011794/how-bike-touring-saved-this-small-town/.
20. Taylor Rojek, "Gravel Rides Are Saving Small-Town America," *Bicycling*, August 8, 2018, https://www.bicycling.com/rides/a22652025/gravel-rides-are-saving-smalltown-america/.

21. Natalie Villwock-Witte and Karalyn Clouser, "Case Studies of Communities of Less than 10,000 People with Bicycle and Pedestrian Infrastructure," Western Transportation Institute, February 2022, https://westerntransportationinstitute.org/wp-content/uploads/2022/03/4W8711_4W8713_SURTCOM_BikePed_CaseStudies_Final-Draft_2022-03-02.pdf.

Conclusion: The Path to the Bicycle City

1. Dylan Walsh, "How Many Americans Are Really Working Remotely?," MIT Sloan School of Management, June 29, 2023, https://mitsloan.mit.edu/ideas-made-to-matter/how-many-americans-are-really-working-remotely.
2. *Economist*, "How to Save Cities from a Death Spiral," June 22, 2023, https://www.economist.com/podcasts/2023/06/22/how-to-save-cities-from-a-death-spiral.
3. Taylor McNeil, "Urban Doom Loop: What It Is and How Cities Can Stop It," Tufts Now, August 16, 2023, https://now.tufts.edu/2023/08/16/urban-doom-loop-what-it-and-how-cities-can-stop-it#:~:text=While%20I%20don%27t%20see,tax-diminishes%2C%200ften%20rapidly.
4. Alex Fitzpatrick, "E-Bike Incentive Programs Are Spreading Nationwide," Axios, August 14, 2023, https://www.axios.com/2023/08/14/e-bike-incentive-program-map.
5. Peter Flax, "Molly's Last Ride," *Bicycling*, January 31, 2023, https://www.bicycling.com/culture/a42690937/molly-steinsapir-lawsuit-rad-power-electric-bike/.
6. Becky Sullivan, "What's Driving the Battery Fires with e-Bikes and Scooters?," National Public Radio, March 11, 2023, https://www.npr.org/2023/03/11/1162732820/e-bike-scooter-lithium-ion-battery-fires.
7. Ash Lovell, "What You Should Know about e-Bike Battery Certification," PeopleForBikes, June 13, 2023, https://www.peopleforbikes.org/news/what-you-should-know-about-e-bike-battery-certification.
8. Thorin Klosowski, "What You Should Know about Right to Repair,"

New York Times, July 15, 2021, https://www.nytimes.com/wirecutter/blog/what-is-right-to-repair/.
9. Maddie Stone-Grist, "E-Bike Companies Are Fighting to Be Exempted from Right-to-Repair Laws," Fast Company, August 10, 2023, https://www.fastcompany.com/90935615/e-bike-companies-are-fighting-to-be-exempted-from-right-to-repair-laws.
10. David Shepardson, "U.S. Lawmakers Introduce 'Right to Repair' Bills to Spur Competition," Reuters, February 3, 2022, https://www.reuters.com/world/us/us-lawmakers-introduce-right-repair-bills-spur-competition-2022-02-03/.
11. European Commission, "Right to Repair: Commission Introduces New Consumer Rights for Easy and Attractive Repairs," press release, March 22, 2023, https://ec.europa.eu/commission/presscorner/detail/en/ip_23_1794.
12. Magnus Lofstrom et al., "Racial Disparities in Traffic Stops," Public Policy Institute of California, October 2022, https://www.ppic.org/publication/racial-disparities-in-traffic-stops/.
13. Smart Growth America, "An Active Roadmap: Best Practices in Rural Mobility," July 27, 2023, https://smartgrowthamerica.org/rural-roadmap/.
14. Smart Growth America, "An Active Roadmap."
15. Josephine K. Hazelton-Boyle and Daniel Piatkowski, "How Prior Experience with Automated Technology Impacts Perceptions of Autonomous Vehicles among Midwestern U.S. Farmers," Public Works Management & Policy 29, no. 1 (2024): 81–100, https://doi.org/10.1177/1087724X231174392.
16. Dario Pevec et al., "A Survey-Based Assessment of How Existing and Potential Electric Vehicle Owners Perceive Range Anxiety," Journal of Cleaner Production 276 (December 10, 2020): 122779, https://doi.org/10.1016/j.jclepr0.2020.122779.
17. White House Briefing Room, "Fact Sheet: Biden-Harris Administration Announces New Standards and Major Progress for a Made-in-America National Network of Electric Vehicle Chargers," February 15, 2023, https://www.whitehouse.gov/briefing-room/statements-releases/2023/02/15

/factsheet-biden-harris-administration-announces-new-standards-and-major-progress-fora-made-in-america-national-network-of-electric-vehicle-chargers/#:~:text=Effective%20immediately%2C%20all%20EV%20chargers,occur%20in%20the%20United%20States.

18. Internal Revenue Service, "Credits for New Clean Vehicles Purchased in 2023 or After," accessed October 20, 2023, https://www.irs.gov/credits-deductions/credits-for-new-clean-vehicles-purchased-in-2023-or-after#:~:text=You%20may%20qualify%20for%20a%20credit%20up%20to%20%247%2C500%20under,purchased%20from%202023%20to%202032.

19. Jack Ewing, "In Norway, the Electric Vehicle Future Has Already Arrived," *New York Times*, May 8, 2023, updated September 17, 2023, https://www.nytimes.com/2023/05/08/business/energy-environment/norway-electric-vehicles.html.

20. David Zipper, "Why Norway—the Poster Child for Electric Cars—Is Having Second Thoughts," Vox, October 31, 2023, https://www.vox.com/future-perfect/23939076/norway-electric-vehicle-cars-evs-tesla-oslo.

21. Anine Hartmann and Sarah Abel, "How Oslo Achieved Zero Pedestrian and Bicycle Fatalities, and How Others Can Apply What Worked," *TheCityFix* (blog), October 13, 2020, https://thecityfix.com/blog/how-oslo-achieved-zero-pedestrian-and-bicycle-fatalities-and-how-others-can-apply-what-worked/.

22. Hannah Figg, "Oslo—Promoting Active Transport Modes," Eltis, updated February 5, 2021, https://www.eltis.org/resources/case-studies/oslo-promoting-active-transport-modes#:~:text=The%20initial%20intention%20of%20the,area%20of%20approximately%201.7%20km2.

23. Terje Elvsaas, "How Oslo Reached Vision Zero: Inside the Car-Free Livability Program That Transformed Norway's Capital," *Medium*, October 14, 2020, https://medium.com/vision-zero-cities-journal/how-oslo-reached-vision-zero-b952aed44697.

24. Jayne P. Lambrou, "Questioning Social Sustainability in Oslo," Sciencenorway.no, October 2, 2022, https://partner.sciencenorway.no/cities-environment-nmbu/questioning-social-sustainability-in-oslo/2086721.

25. Maria J. Leirbakk et al., "Look to Norway: Serving New Families and

Infants in a Multiethnic Population," *Infant Mental Health Journal* 40, no. 5 (September–October 2019): 659–72, https://doi.org/10.1002/imhj.21804.

26. Elvsaas, "How Oslo Reached Vision Zero."
27. Jessica Coulon, "Oslo Just Proved Vision Zero Is Possible: The Norwegian Capital Had Zero Pedestrian and Cyclist Fatalities in 2019," *Bicycling*, January 7, 2020, https://www.bicycling.com/news/a30433288/oslo-vision-zero-goal-2019/.
28. Mari Wøien Meijer, "ACPA—Adapting European Cities to Population Ageing: Policy Challenges and Best Practices; Case Study Report: Oslo," ESPON, April 23, 2020, https://www.espon.eu/sites/default/files/attachments/12.%20ACPA_city%20report_Oslo_1.pdf.
29. WHO Global Network for Age-Friendly Cities and Communities, "OSLO: Action Plans for Age-Friendly City and Safe and Diversified Care of Older People; City Government Propositions 174/17 and 175/17," accessed October 20, 2023, https://extranet.who.int/agefriendlyworld/wp-content/uploads/2015/03/Action-plan-age-friendly-Oslo.pdf.
30. Nick Romeo, "How Oslo Learned to Fight Climate Change: Norway's Biggest City Is Charting a Path Forward for the World," *New Yorker*, May 4, 2022, https://www.newyorker.com/news/annals-of-a-warming-planet/how-oslo-learned-to-fight-climate-change.
31. City of Oslo, Climate Department, Agency for Climate, "Greenhouse Gas Inventory for Oslo, 2009–2020," March 30, 2022, https://www.klimaoslo.no/wp-content/uploads/sites/88/2022/10/GHG-inventory-for-Oslo-2020.pdf.
32. Sophie Davies, "COVID-19 Pandemic Puts Barcelona Urban Greening Plan in the Fast Lane," Reuters, January 10, 2021, https://www.reuters.com/article/us-spain-coronavirus-city-environment-fe-idUSKBN29G0I2.
33. Feargus O'Sullivan, "Can Milan Become Europe's Most Bike-Friendly City?," Bloomberg CityLab, January 13, 2022, https://www.bloomberg.com/news/articles/2022-01-14/milan-plans-bike-lane-infrastructure-to-rival-paris.
34. Jamey M. B. Volker and Susan Handy, "Economic Impacts on Local

Businesses of Investments in Bicycle and Pedestrian Infrastructure: A Review of the Evidence," *Transport Reviews* 41, no. 4 (2021): 401–31, https://doi.org/10.1080/01441647.2021.1912849.

35. Daniel P. Piatkowski, Wesley E. Marshall, and Kevin J. Krizek, "Carrots versus Sticks: Assessing Intervention Effectiveness and Implementation Challenges for Active Transport," *Journal of Planning Education and Research* 39, no. 1 (2019): 50–64, https://doi.org/10.1177/0739456X17715306.

36. I first met with Norman more than a decade ago, when we did research led by Wes Marshall studying how suburban sprawl is bad for our health. In that work, we demonstrated that just by looking at the streets, we could predict health. The worst outcomes were associated with the disconnected loops and curves of suburban development. Alternatively, people living in neighborhoods with denser, more connected streets and small blocks were generally healthier. That work, now a decade old, challenged me to think beyond bicycle promotion and to consider how myriad components of our built environments interact to affect (in this case) our health.

37. Monica Menendez and Lukas Ambühl, "Implementing Design and Operational Measures for Sustainable Mobility: Lessons from Zurich," *Sustainability* 14, no. 2 (2022): 625, https://doi.org/10.3390/su14020625.

38. Joseph Dodds, "The Psychology of Climate Anxiety," *BJPsych Bulletin* 45, no. 4 (2021): 222–26, https://doi.org/10.1192/bjb.2021.18; erratum in *BJPsych Bulletin* 45, no. 4 (2021): 256, https://doi.org/10.1192/bjb.2021.58.

39. Rebecca Leber, "3 Years Ago, We All Laughed at James Inhofe's Snowball. The Joke Was on Us," *Mother Jones*, February 26, 2018, https://www.motherjones.com/environment/2018/02/3-years-ago-we-all-laughed-at-james-inhofes-snowball-the-joke-was-onus/.

40. Grant Ennis, *Dark PR: How Corporate Disinformation Harms Our Health and the Environment* (Wakefield, Quebec: Daraja Press, 2023).

41. Donald C. Shoup, *The High Cost of Free Parking* (London: Routledge, 2011).

42. Jonathan Levine, *Zoned Out: Regulation, Markets, and Choices in*

Transportation and Metropolitan Land-Use (Washington, DC: Resources for the Future, 2005).
43. Timothy Welch, "Electric Cars Alone Won't Save the Planet. We'll Need to Design Cities So People Can Walk and Cycle Safely," The Conversation, November 16, 2021, https://theconversation.com/electric-cars-alone-wont-save-the-planet-well-need-to-design-cities-so-people-can-walk-and-cycle-safely-171818.
44. Ralph Buehler, "Can Public Transportation Compete with Automated and Connected Cars?," *Journal of Public Transportation* 21, no. 1 (2018): 7–18, https://doi.org/10.5038/2375-0901.21.1.2.
45. Melissa Bruntlett and Chris Bruntlett, *Building the Cycling City: The Dutch Blueprint for Urban Vitality* (Washington, DC: Island Press, 2018).
46. Mikael Colville-Andersen, *Copenhagenize: The Definitive Guide to Global Bicycle Urbanism* (Washington, DC: Island Press, 2018).
47. Ennis, *Dark PR*.
48. Dan Baer, "How to Break Polarizing Gridlock? Push for Big, Popular Change," Carnegie Endowment for International Peace, November 20, 2020, https://carnegieendowment.org/2020/11/20/how-to-break-polarizing-gridlock-push-for-big-popular-change-pub-83291.
49. Williams Lyons et al., "Nonmotorized Transportation Pilot Program: Continued Progress in Developing Walking and Bicycling Networks—May 2014," Repository and Open Science Access Portal, May 1, 2014, https://rosap.ntl.bts.gov/view/dot/12063.
50. County of Marin (California), Department of Public Works, "Cal Park Hill Tunnel: Rehabilitation and Multi-Use Pathway Project," accessed October 20, 2023, https://www.walkbikemarin.org/documents/Fact_Sheets/CalPark_brochure_12-10.pdf.
51. Julia Belluz, "Why Minneapolis Was Voted the Most Bike-Friendly City in America," Vox, December 3, 2015, https://www.vox.com/2015/12/3/9843562/minneapolis-bike-friendly.
52. National Institute for Transportation and Communities, "Barriers to Biking for Women and Minorities," NITC Project Brief, May 2017, https://ppms.trec.pdx.edu/media/project_files/Friedly_994_Marginalized_Cyclists.pdf.

53. tamika l. butler, "Why We Must Talk about Race When We Talk about Bikes," *Bicycling*, June 9, 2020, https://www.bicycling.com/culture/a32783551/cycling-talk-fight-racism/.
54. Kiran Herbert, "5 Strategies Every Bike Advocate Needs," PeopleForBikes, accessed January 15, 2024, https://www.peopleforbikes.org/news/5-strategies-every-bike-advocate-needs.
55. Centers for Disease Control and Prevention, "The Community Preventive Services Task Force's Built Environment Recommendation to Increase Physical Activity," accessed October 20, 2023, https://www.cdc.gov/physicalactivity/downloads/built-environment-recommendation.pdf.
56. US Department of Transportation, Federal Highway Administration, "The Environmental Benefits of Bicycling and Walking: Case Study No. 15," Publication No. FHWA-PD-93-015, January 1993, https://safety.fhwa.dot.gov/ped_bike/docs/case15.pdf.
57. Daniel Piatkowski, Wesley Marshall, and Nader Afzalan, "Can Web-Based Community Engagement Inform Equitable Planning Outcomes? A Case Study of Bikesharing," *Journal of Urbanism: International Research on Placemaking and Urban Sustainability* 10, no. 3 (2017): 296–309, https://doi.org/10.1080/17549175.2016.1254672; Trisalyn Nelson et al., "Crowdsourced Data for Bicycling Research and Practice," *Transport Reviews* 41, no. 1 (2021): 97–114, https://doi.org/10.1080/01441647.2020.1806943.
58. Thomas Elliott and Jennifer Earl, "Online Protest Participation and the Digital Divide: Modeling the Effect of the Digital Divide on Online Petition-Signing," *New Media & Society* 20, no. 2 (2018): 698–719, https://doi.org/10.1177/1461444816669159.
59. Greg P. Griffin and Junfeng Jiao, "Crowdsourcing Bike Share Station Locations," *Journal of the American Planning Association* 85, no. 1 (2019): 35–48, https://doi.org/10.1080/01944363.2018.1476174.
60. Sara Meerow, Pani Pajouhesh, and Thaddeus R. Miller, "Social Equity in Urban Resilience Planning," *Local Environment* 24, no. 9 (2019): 793–808, https://doi.org/10.1080/13549839.2019.1645103.
61. Daniel Piatkowski et al., "Measuring the Impacts of Bike-to-Work Day

Events and Identifying Barriers to Increased Commuter Cycling," technical paper, *Journal of Urban Planning and Development* 141, no. 4 (August 13, 2014), https://doi.org/10.1061/(ASCE)UP.1943-5444.0000239.

62. Nathaniel Minor, "Denver Parents Encourage Physical Activity and Fun with a Project Called: Bike Bus," National Public Radio, *Morning Edition*, September 22, 2023, https://www.npr.org/2023/09/22/1200998511/denver-parents-encourage-physical-activity-and-fun-with-a-project-called-bike-bu.

63. Donnie Johnson Sackey, "Without Permission: Guerrilla Gardening, Contested Places, Spatial Justice," *Review of Communication* 22, no. 4 (2022): 364–77, https://doi.org/10.1080/15358593.2022.2133970.

64. Krzysztof Herman and Maria Rodgers, "From Tactical Urbanism Action to Institutionalised Urban Planning and Educational Tool: The Evolution of Park(ing) Day," *Land* 9, no. 7 (2020): 217, https://doi.org/10.3390/land9070217.

65. "Park(ing) Day," accessed September 21, 2023, https://www.myparkingday.org.

66. National Association of City Transportation Officials, "Design Guidance," accessed September 21, 2023, https://nacto.org/program/design-guidance/.

67. Donald Shoup, "How Parking Requirements Hurt the Poor," *Washington Post*, March 3, 2016, https://www.washingtonpost.com/news/in-theory/wp/2016/03/03/how-parking-requirements-hurt-the-poor/#.

68. Karen Chapple et al., "Jumpstarting the Market for Accessory Dwelling Units: Lessons Learned from Portland, Seattle, and Vancouver," University of California, Berkeley, 2017, https://escholarship.org/uc/item/4b9836bh.

Epilogue

1. Statens Vegvesen, "National Plan of Action for Road Safety, 2022–2025," August 24, 2022, https://www.vegvesen.no/globalassets/fag/fokusomrader/trafikksikkerhet/national-plan-of-action-for-road-safety-2022-2025---short-version-in-english.pdf.

2. Karin Edvardsson Björnberg et al., eds., *The Vision Zero Handbook:*

Theory, Technology, and Management for a Zero Casualty Policy (Cham, Switzerland: Springer, 2023).
3. Jessie Singer, *There Are No Accidents: The Deadly Rise of Injury and Disaster—Who Profits and Who Pays the Price* (New York: Simon & Schuster, 2023).
4. Rebecca B. Naumann et al., "Systems Thinking in the Context of Road Safety: Can Systems Tools Help Us Realize a True 'Safe Systems' Approach?," *Current Epidemiology Reports* 7 (October 1, 2020): 343–51, https://doi.org/10.1007/s40471-020-00248-z.
5. Beate Elvebakk, "Vision Zero: Remaking Road Safety," *Mobilities* 2, no. 3 (2007): 425–41, https://doi.org/10.1080/17450100701597426.
6. Statistisk Sentralbyrå (Statistics Norway), https://www.ssb.no.
7. US Department of Transportation, National Highway Traffic Safety Administration, https://www.nhtsa.gov.
8. Kirstine Lund Christiansen and IngeMerete Hougaard, "Copenhagen Was Supposed to Be the Climate Leader. What Happened?," *Fast Company*, September 14, 2022, https://www.fastcompany.com/90789415/copenhagen-was-supposed-to-be-the-climate-leader-what-happened.
9. Carbon Neutral Cities Alliance, https://carbonneutralcities.org.
10. City of Oslo, Norway, "Climate Strategy for Oslo towards 2030: Short Version," August 2020, https://www.klimaoslo.no/wp-content/uploads/sites/88/2020/09/Klimastrategi2030-Kortversjon-ENG_2608_enkeltside.pdf.
11. Andrew E. MacNeily, "What's Past Is Prologue," *Canadian Urological Association Journal* 14, no. 4 (2020): 81, https://doi.org/10.5489/cuaj.6497.

ABOUT THE AUTHOR

Dan Piatkowski is an American academic and urban planner based in Oslo, Norway, where he is on the faculty at OsloMet—Oslo Metropolitan University. Before moving to Norway, Dan worked in some area of urban planning (either academic or professional) in Colorado, Arizona, New Mexico, Nebraska, and Georgia.

Dan got his start in the bike world in the early 2000s with a very brief stint as a bicycle messenger in New York City before finding his way to working at bike shops, riding all kinds of bikes, and getting active in bicycle advocacy.

These days, he spends more time writing about bicycles than riding them. Dan is the author of many articles and cowrote the book *Bicycling for Transportation: An Evidence-Base for Communities.*